The Block Book

Third Edition

Elisabeth S. Hirsch, Editor

National Association for the Education of Young Children
Washington, D.C.

Photographs

Nancy P. Alexander—91; Ellen Galinsky—front cover, 3, 6, 29, 34, 51, 59, 67, 130 (left), 142, 143; Peter Glass—76; Jean-Claude LeJeune—145; Lois Lord—64, 106; Marietta Lynch—36, 43, 85, 146; Lois Main—28; Susan May—109; Anne-Marie Mott—30, 31, 38 (left & right), 45 (top & bottom), 54, 62, 72 (top, middle, & bottom), 78 (left & right), 83, 88, 94, 99, 112, 118, 121, 123, 130 (right), 133, 136, 138, 146, 147 (left & right), 148; Francis Wardle—69, 127, 144

Drawings

Susan Hirsch—Chapter 8, Appendix 2; Harriet M. Johnson—Chapter 2 (used by permission of Bank Street College of Education Publications); Kristina Leeb-Lundberg—Chapter 4; Scientific Illustrators—134, 135; Melanie Rose White—119

National Association for the Education
  of Young Children
1313 L Street, NW, Suite 500
Washington DC 20005-4101
202-232-8777 or 800-424-2460
www.naeyc.org

Through its publications program the National Association for the Education of Young Children (NAEYC) provides a forum for discussion of major issues and ideas in the early childhood field, with the hope of provoking thought and promoting professional growth. The views expressed or implied are not necessarily those of the Association.

Library of Congress Catalog Card Number: 84-60160
ISBN 0-935989-76-5
NAEYC #132

Editor (of third edition): Carol Copple; *Design and production:* Jack Zibulsky and Angela S. Dixon; *Editorial assistance:* Betty Nylund Barr, Sandi Collins, Anika Trahan, and Penny Atkins.

Printed in the United States of America

Contents

About the Editor

Elisabeth S. Hirsch, Ph.D., was a teacher of preschoolers in independent private schools and parent cooperatives for many years. She was director of a parent cooperative and a day care center. At the same time, she worked extensively with parent groups, leading study groups and parent meetings.

Elisabeth Hirsch received her education at Teachers College, Columbia University; the New School for Social Research; and New York University. On the faculty of the City University of New York since 1968, she retired from its City College in 1988. Now, as a professor emerita, she continues teaching at City College and working as a consultant.

Dr. Hirsch has published *Problems of Early Childhood* and numerous articles and pamphlets.

Contributors

Charlotte Brody was the principal of the lower division of the Little Red Schoolhouse in New York and a consultant to the Day Care Unit of the New York City Department of Health. She has had experience in teaching and directing preschools. She now works part-time at Brooklyn College of the City University of New York, as well as doing consulting work.

Sally Cartwright, as a child in the 1930s, worked with blocks at City and Country School (C&C), often under the lively, discerning eye of Caroline Pratt. Over the next few decades she earned a master's degree from Bank Street College of Education and taught in rural and urban, public and private settings, including C&C. She eventually started her own small, experimental preschool in Maine, where both unit blocks and large blocks were central to children's learning.

Harriet K. Cuffaro is on the graduate faculty of the Bank Street College of Education, New York City. She taught at the City and Country School, the Child Development

Center in New York City, and in the public schools of California.

Elizabeth Dreier is the principal of the Murray Avenue School in Larchmont, New York. She was coordinator of the Lower School of the New Lincoln School in New York City, administrator of the Walden School, and faculty member of City College, City University of New York.

Harriet M. Johnson came to early childhood education from a rich background in public health, teaching, and settlement work. In 1917 she planned an "educational experiment for young children" which she called "The Nursery School," one of the first in the United States. This school became the demonstration program of the Bank Street College of Education. Miss Johnson was the school's director and a Bank Street faculty member until her death in 1934.

Kristina Leeb-Lundberg, professor emerita of City College, City University of New York, has specialized on the intellectual level of preschool block building. She wrote a pathbreaking thesis on Froebel that bridged European and U.S. early education, and her publications in English, German, and Spanish have stressed a creative and dynamic approach to mathematics in the lives of young children. Dr. Leeb-Lundberg has been an invited speaker at several international early childhood and mathematics congresses.

Lucy Sprague Mitchell (1878–1967) devoted her long and productive life to the education of children and their teachers. She was founder and later president of the Bank Street College of Education. She was also the author of material for teachers in early childhood and elementary education and is probably best known for her milestone contributions to children's literature.

Mary W. Moffitt is professor emerita of Queens College, City University of New York. She is the author of numerous articles and books dealing with early childhood and science education. She was consultant on the film *Blocks, a Medium for Perceptual Learning* (Campus Films) and is author of the video-cassette-slide program *Block Building* (Childhood Resources).

Charlotte B. Winsor, for many years director of the Graduate Program Division of Bank Street College of Education, served at that college as archivist and Distinguished Teacher Education Specialist until her death in 1983. She was the author of many books and pamphlets and a teacher at the City and Country School at the time when the concepts of block building originated and developed there.

Preface

As a young teacher, I once met an acquaintance I had not seen in years. "What do you do?" she asked.

"I teach."

"What do you teach?"

"Nursery school."

The lady looked a little puzzled.

"*What* do you teach in nursery school?"

I must admit that I had no ready answer. Seeing my embarrassment, she quickly provided a reply for me.

"Oh, I know, *nursery rhymes!*"

It probably would have been less awkward for me had I answered, "I help children learn." But even here the stumbling block comes with the next question: "Learn *what?*"

This book attempts to provide a partial answer: mathematics, science, social studies—respectable disciplines, as they are furthered through block building. The full truth, however, lies elsewhere. The disciplines as we know them are arbitrary divisions of human understanding. Certainly, young children gain experiential foundations that enable them to build understandings of a verbal, abstract nature in later years.

Certainly, teachers must know and *must know how to tell others* that these activities are vital and why this is so.

Let us not put the cart before the horse, however. What we provide with blocks is experience with a material, combining structure and freedom in a felicitous way.

The pure geometrical forms of unit blocks remind us of Edna St. Vincent Millay's line, "Euclid alone has looked on bare beauty." The pleasure of blocks stems primarily from the aesthetic experience. It involves the whole person—muscles and senses, intellect and emotion, individual growth and social interaction. Learning results from the imaginative activity, from the need to pose and solve problems.

According to Piaget, cognitive growth occurs through physical maturation coupled with firsthand experience.

Blocks further these processes.

This volume examines in detail some of these aspects of learning through block building. One book could never encompass all of the potential for learning.

—*Elisabeth S. Hirsch*

Potential Contributions of Blocks for Early Childhood Curriculum*

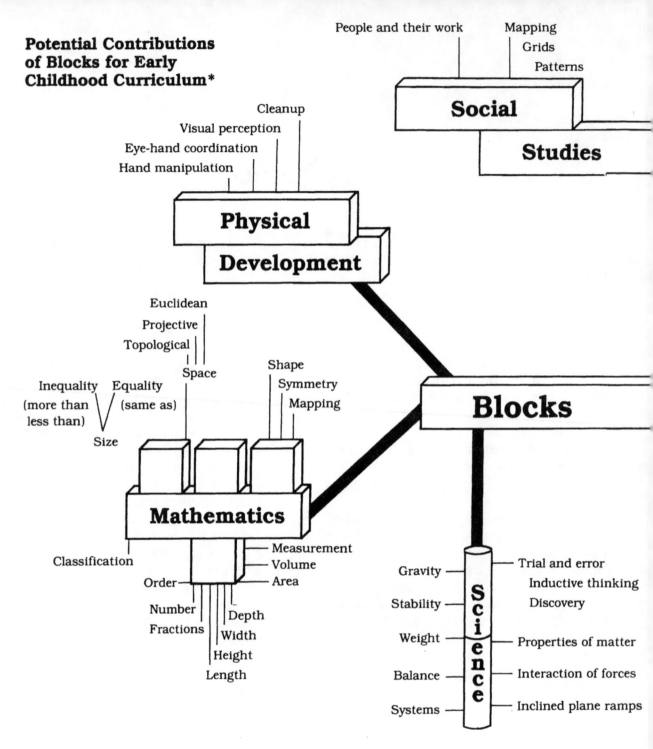

*Adapted from Charlotte Brody.
The Block Book, edited by Elisabeth S. Hirsch
National Association for the Education of Young Children

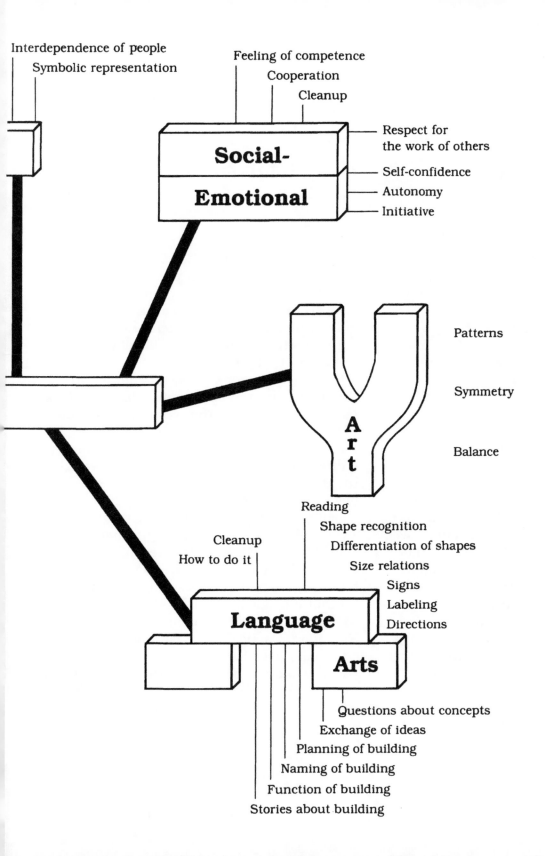

Interdependence of people

Symbolic representation

Feeling of competence

Cooperation

Cleanup

Social-Emotional

Respect for the work of others

Self-confidence

Autonomy

Initiative

Patterns

Symmetry

Balance

Art

Reading

Shape recognition

Differentiation of shapes

Size relations

Signs

Labeling

Directions

Cleanup

How to do it

Language Arts

Questions about concepts

Exchange of ideas

Planning of building

Naming of building

Function of building

Stories about building

ix

Introduction
To the Third Edition

It has been more than 20 years since *The Block Book* was first published. I hope that this book contributed to the revival of block building in classrooms.

The early childhood scene has changed tremendously in the last 20 years. As women entered the workforce in overwhelming numbers and as massive funding provided the means, both the need for and the availability of preschool classes increased manifold.

Due to the shift in funding and funders' demand for accountability and for "outcomes," or possibly the increased emphasis on cognition and skill learning that forced teachers to plan more and worry more about demonstrable learning, there has been a shift in teacher attitudes about children's play. We must find a way to support children's initiative, curiosity, and their built-in potential for growth and learning. Teachers' plans, goals, and support, if appropriate, can stimulate and enrich children's spontaneous invention.

The challenge to the teacher is to find ways to alter plans that did not turn out to be fruitful and to document the learning and growth achieved. In an addition to her chapter (beginning on p. 75), Harriet Cuffaro discusses these issues and provides thought-provoking illustrations.

This new edition of *The Block Book* contains many changes yet preserves many old favorites. Once again we present, in its entirety, Harriet Johnson's timeless discussion of blocks as an aesthetic experience, which includes an introduction by Lucy Sprague Mitchell.

Charlotte Winsor's powerful chapter on Caroline Pratt and on learning through block building reminds us that serious appreciation of hands-on learning preceded Piaget.

Also unchanged are Mary Moffitt's chapter on the growth of scientific thinking through the use of blocks and Elizabeth Dreier's discussion of the way blocks can enhance learning in the primary grades.

Several chapters have gone through revisions to make them more accessible and current. The chapter by Kristina Leeb-Lundberg on mathematics, the chapter by Charlotte Brody and Elisabeth Hirsch on social studies, and the chapter by Elisabeth Hirsch on practical considerations in the classroom have been extensively revised.

A new chapter by Sally Cartwright, adapted from an article for *Young Children*, discusses large hollow blocks. Large blocks allow children to physically enter their buildings rather than to simply view them from the outside.

This leads to dramatic-play experiences that provide understandings of a different nature, although not a less important one. The recognition of this medium extends this volume and highlights another fruitful facet of children's activities.

Manipulatives of the table-block variety have not been included, although the construction problems they raise and the learnings they provide are often identical to those of unit blocks. While table activities are important, children younger than 6 should not be expected to sit at tables anymore than is necessary. Here again, we take our cue from children. Active children move their whole bodies; they investigate and explore the world and their role in it; they sort out feelings and experiences through play.

As illustrated by the chart at the front of this book, block building challenges the whole child. It builds self-confidence; it enhances social skills; it facilitates vocabulary development; and it stimulates eye-hand-body coordination, so important for the development of reading skills. In addition, it enriches the traditional subjects of the curriculum—mathematics, science, and social studies. As they build with blocks, children discover, invent, imagine, and construct a fuller understanding of their world.

—*Elisabeth S. Hirsch*
June 1996

Acknowledgments

My grateful acknowledgments are due first and foremost to my husband Julius E. Hirsch, who believed in me and in this work. He supported me both spiritually and with his two typing fingers.

I wish to thank Anne-Marie Mott, director of the Lower School of the Bank Street School for Children. Anne-Marie fortuitously combines knowledge of children with a photographer's skill. Most of the new pictures in this edition are due to her special effort.

Last but not least, my thanks and admiration to NAEYC staff members Carol Copple, Betty Nylund Barr, Sandi Collins, Jack Zibulsky, and Angela Dixon. The editorial staff combined editorial skill with real concern for content and respect for the various contributors. No easy task.

—*E.S.H.*

1

Blocks as a Material for Learning through Play

Charlotte B. Winsor

The contribution of Caroline Pratt

Through the years, there has been much elaboration and interpretation of blocks as a material and block play as a learning method in early childhood education. Because Caroline Pratt's work has long been associated with the development of the basic unit blocks, I have found it useful to seek out her early writings (Pratt 1924, 1948, 1973) and, together with personal recall, attempt to share her thinking about the role of this material in children's learning.

Caroline Pratt was born in 1867 in Fayetteville, a small town in upper New York state. Her childhood and growing years are so much a prototype of rural society in 19th century America and so much written about in story and statistic that they hardly need much further development here. Her lifetime spanned a bursting technology of such magnitude that she recalls, "I remember the day we all went down to the store to see my mother make our first call on the telephone. . . ." And before she was old, Lucy Sprague Mitchell would write

> Modern children are born into an appallingly complicated world. A three-year-old in a city environment may be whisked to his steam-heated nursery in an electric elevator, fed from supplies which are ordered by telephone, sent up in a dumbwaiter, and stored in an electric refrigerator; he may be taken to a hole in the sidewalk and borne rapidly on an underground train to a distant place. The forces which move his elevator, warm his nursery, extend his mother's voice to a grocery store, cool his milk, propel the subway train, are complicated and difficult to understand not only at three, at six, at nine, but even at forty. (Mitchell [1921] 1971, 12)

And this before the advent of the atomic era, TV, and computers! It is hardly to be wondered then that thoughtful people, then as now, were reassessing the role of the school or that Miss Pratt, with others, was seeking an environment in which children could find appropriate experiences beyond the simple routines of learning to read, write, and reckon.

Similarly, the making of a teacher (teacher education as a professional enterprise was in an embryonic stage at the time) has been expressed tersely, "I pinned up my braids, and there I was—a teacher." For Miss Pratt, it was her great-uncle Homer who said, "Carrie was always good with children," and so, at 16 she became the one teacher in a one-room school in a nearby town. In her words, "I next taught first grade in our village school, and when the children and I were thoroughly weary of the 3R's I varied the program by teaching the little boys to tip their hats to a woman" (Pratt 1948, xii). Her teaching style, primitive as it must have been, aroused sufficient interest in the community to get her an offer of a scholarship to Teachers College in New York.

There she went to begin a lifelong rebellion with traditional methods in education and to search for the meanings in learning that led eventually to the field of childhood education. She was not a happy student, nor a shining light in the courses in kindergarten education to which she was exposed, sensing as she did that much of the content and method of the program might keep the teacher happy, but was hardly of service to the young child's growth needs or capacities. So she turned to manual training, a favorite innovation in education of the 1890s. But again, she found an emptiness of childhood purpose in the exercises she had to master in order that she might pass them on to the children she would teach.

Her first formal teaching assignment, however, was in the manual training shop in a normal school, where, as she put it, she was "teaching young women to saw to a line." Obviously, she found this nonproductive in her quest and turned to further exploration. In Sweden at this time, there had been developed a school of manual training that moved from performing exercises to making models, and here Miss Pratt went to study at the Sloyd School, only to return with her models, useless to her and certainly meaningless to children.

But she was also studying, reaching out for guidance in new ways of teaching, and attempting the most difficult of all tasks—to formulate an original concept of education, "an exploration into the world of children and their ways of growing and learning." It was in these years also that broader concepts of education began to take shape. Social consciousness, aroused by contact with workers and radicals of many schools of thought, became another thread in the pattern of her thinking. Education as a lifelong undertaking for the individual and a force in molding a better world took shape for her.

It was at the turn of the century that Miss Pratt came to live and work in New York City. Here in settlement houses and in one small school, she began to teach real children and to apply some of the principles which had been gestating for some years. She was already convinced that in the process of children's play was the germ of serious learning, indeed a major rehearsal for the tasks awaiting them in growing up.

But such a concept of learning and teaching called for, among other things, the *materials* with which to play. The components of

Blocks remain simply pieces of wood unless they are infused with information gleaned from experience.

play settings were needed in which children's amorphous ideas could be formulated, dramatized, and perhaps later become accurate statements of reality. Miss Pratt, building on her skills in woodworking, undertook a toy making enterprise, expecting in her naive exuberance to revolutionize education by this backdoor entrance. Her efforts came to nothing at the time, but an approach to early childhood experience through the medium of play materials—toys—remained a basic element of her work.

A first opportunity to try out her ideas and such toys was simply a bare space in a settlement house, where she was permitted a 2-month period for her experiment. She volunteered to provide the materials, find the children, and develop a program. To provide the obvious kindergarten materials was a simple task. She was seeking something more—the wherewithal with which children could re-create their experiences. She had seen and admired the Patty Hill blocks in the kindergarten at Teachers College. But she was seeking a material more flexible and adaptable, that would afford a base line for teaching and learning. She was searching for a truly serious approach to children's play, more than simple playing with blocks in free time. She believed that teachers could provide richer content for play through the experiences they offered children.

It was for this settlement house experiment that Miss Pratt planned what was to become her design for an early childhood classroom. In her words,

> There were the blocks I had made, and the toys I designed and made myself; there were the crayons and papers and there was clay . . . I had made it as easy and inviting as I knew how, and then I stood aside and let them forage for themselves.

One of the six 5-year-olds whom she had recruited for her program put her theory about childhood play into practice.

> I couldn't have asked for a more appropriate demonstration of my belief in the serious value of children's play. Michael was so deeply absorbed . . . he might have been a scientist working out an experiment in a laboratory . . . . With blocks to help him, he was using all his mental powers, reasoning out relationships . . . and drawing conclusions. He was learning to think. (Pratt 1948, 31–32)

The results of this brief experiment would have been frustrating, as well as exhilarating, had it not been for an offer of further support for her work. Once more, Miss Pratt found a few 5-year-olds whose parents were ready to let her play school with them. Her name for this undertaking was indeed the Play School, but with vastly deeper meanings for her.

Her emphasis from here onward seemed to turn toward the development of a body of content that children could build upon in their play. Their idiosyncratic expression of experience was valued, at least theoretically. For one child, a trip to the docks—a much used learning center in this little school—might be expressed in blocks as a rather accurate representation of an ocean liner; while for another, a large expanse of blue paint on paper might re-create the experience of the vast river. But, basically, to build knowledge about the world in which one lives, and with the autonomy and the tools (materials, among which blocks held high priority) with which to express such knowledge, was at the crux of this method.

It is interesting to note that nowhere in Miss Pratt's writings is there a specific reference to the invention of the unit blocks that came to be associated with her name. In fact, many years later, when her beloved City and Country School was in dire financial straits, and it was suggested that the blocks be patented, she resisted angrily, insisting that blocks would remain simply pieces of wood unless infused with a body of information which is gleaned from experience.

Writing some years later in a description of the Play School, she offers her premise.

> Toys and blocks do not respond to the need of a child who has no related knowledge to fall back upon. If a child does not know that a horse's home is a stable, where he is fed and cared for, if he does not know the

use either of a horse or a wagon, it is useless to present him with a horse and wagon to play with. (in Winsor 1973, 28)

Such experience for the New York City child may seem quaint today, but her principle of play as learning experience is stated explicitly. One must also infer the active role of the adult in providing experience appropriate to age level needs and the furthering of primary experience by discussion, materials, and analysis, if one may use the term.

And in this statement is embodied, more than blocks as a material for play, a philosophy of learning with play as its springboard. Miss Pratt believed that children perceive their need for enriched information, not per se, not to gratify the adult's wish to teach them, but in order to enhance the quality of their play. They raise new inquiries that carry on to the discovery of further intellectual relationships. An example may be in order here. Children build boats, especially in a seaport city. In an early stage of the child's development, some essential physical characteristics are presented, the shape of the boat, the sounds it makes. But then the questions come. *Where does it go? How do people get to land?* Then, *What is a dock?* Further, *What is the boat carrying? Who makes it go?* And, still later, *What are the essentials of transportation in the real world?* The sensitive skill of the teacher is called upon to nurture appropriate questions and answers with the children and, most important, to provide experience within which children may find answers for themselves. And the new knowledge pays its own dividend, namely, more fun in their play world. One may hypothesize that by such methods, children find the very quest for knowledge a gratifying experience, and the learning process moves.

The implementation in depth of much of Miss Pratt's theoretical stance became possible with the founding and growth of the City and Country School. Together with Harriet Johnson and Lucy Sprague Mitchell, she was able to recruit numbers of children, observe them in the hands of specially prepared teachers over long periods of time (from infancy to adolescence), and record behavior in group and individual experiences. Miss Johnson's formulation, arrived at from exhaustive recording and study of very young children's use of blocks, offers three major points of emphasis: first, "the power to deal effectively with his environment accrues to a child through the free use of constructive material"; second, "possibilities are offered by blocks and similar materials for expressing rhythm, pattern, design"; and third, "by means of these materials, children may review, rehearse and play out their past experience" (Johnson [1928] 1972, 183–89).

In these deceptively simple statements, one finds a structure that encompasses the major principles of child growth. What is meant by that first statement and where does its import take us? Children's strength lies in their vigorous need for action, leading on to a grasping for competence. This they can best achieve by mastery of appropriate materials. Miss Pratt carries such thinking further in stating one of her fervent beliefs, "The unfortunate child is the one who has his interest riveted in people, because he cannot manage them, convert them to his purposes. They dominate him and he is converted to their purposes" (Pratt 1924, 5).

Blocks offer an almost infinite variety of expressive opportunity, from simple designs to veritable engineering feats of bridge building.

In many schools, blocks are a basic material for the older children in the nursery years. For them, there develop more elaborate expectations, a further intellectual (academic) exploitation of the possible learnings. As has been indicated earlier, the content of children's play—information about reality—was viewed as an essential ingredient when such play is seen as having a major role in the learning process. The facts of our world and its workings become the scripts for the dramas played out in block schemes, as they are called. Such a scheme demands preplanning, group organization with specialization of tasks, buildings sufficiently true to reality to serve as settings and sturdily engineered to withstand real play.

The second statement tells us that such materials serve, by their very freedom, more than the realistic purpose of re-creating the known. The young child who laid down blocks rhythmically, decorated the structure fancifully, and named it "just a sign" tells us that these seemingly plain materials can become a veritable artist's palette for some children.

The third statement comes very close to a definition of play offered many years later by Erikson, who proposes a theory "that the child's play is the infantile form of human ability to deal with experience by creating model situations and to master reality by experimenting and planning" (1950, 195).

For this author, remembrances of such block schemes fill the mind. One such experience may be worth a description. Upon a return from a trip to a nearby building site, one child drew a primitive floor plan on a large piece of paper. Dramatically, he unrolled this before his companions and directed them to their various building jobs. Only then did the teacher recall seeing the supervisor on the job using a blueprint with the workers. And it should be added this was only the beginning of a play scheme that lasted several days and was elaborated as the children built the structure, dramatized the functions of the builders, and finally drew into their play other children to be tenants of their building.

The opportunity for social studies content arising from such block play boggles the mind and needs to be used judiciously, lest one forget the axiom of readiness for receiving stimuli. And one could make as good a case for math or science or reading. But others will undertake to discuss these aspects of blocks as a material in early childhood programs.

Another question, much pondered, is what supplementary materials best serve block play. Here Caroline Pratt was, at least to this author, an absolute purist. No reason to provide a car, an animal, or a truck when the child could improvise or make a crude replica of a needed object, said she. In fact, one deep virtue for her in this material was the way it led children to creativity with other materials—e.g., wood to fashion a car, clay to model a figure, paints or crayon to indicate a needed river or street. Supplementary materials therefore should be adaptable to a variety of uses—cloth, bits of wire or hose, or oddly shaped pieces of wood, the springs of an old clock, or whatever the ingenuity of the teacher brought to the class to stimulate the imagination toward an original solution of a problem in the children's constructions. The settings she valued were austere to the point of barrenness, yet, somehow, presenting children with a clarity of choice and becoming with time real workshops for children. How sharply such settings contrast with many of our nursery classrooms today, often filled with commercial products so finished as to dictate their use with little adaptability to the child's imaginative purposes.

Perhaps, inevitably, children, as all of us, are living in a world further than ever removed from the primary processes of their existence. Whether the school can or should attempt to bring to the child opportunities for unraveling some of our complexities is a baffling imponderable.

Only faith in the children themselves and the prime importance of play as their mode of experimentation and discovery can offer a base for further exploration of the true value of the materials in the programs of early childhood education.

One may summarize the body of principles that have governed this approach to childhood learning in the following statements:

• The child needs an autonomous and active role in the learning process.

• Play is the process by which the child's experience is expressed and organized.

• Play is enriched as further experience including primary and vicarious information becomes available.

• Development of play requires adaptable materials that can serve fantasy as well as reality experience.

• Blocks offer an almost infinite variety of expressive opportunity from floor patterns or designs to veritable engineering feats of bridge building. But blocks remain a means rather than an end in the learning process.

• Children can achieve true mastery of adaptable materials in their own terms and know the gratification of competence at their level of maturity without dependence upon adult judgment of a given product.

• The teaching role becomes complementary to the process—providing, enriching, leading on to further experience.

• Beyond any material lies the need for adult understanding of the child's maturity level and growth, which becomes the base line upon which materials and experience are provided.

References

Erikson, E.H. 1950. *Childhood and society.* New York: Norton.

Johnson, H. 1972. *Children in the nursery school.* New York: Agathon. Reissued with an introductory essay by Barbara Biber.

Mitchell, L.S. [1921] 1971. *Young geographers.* New York: Agathon.

Pratt, C., ed. 1924. *Experimental practice in the City and Country School.* New York: E.P. Dutton.

Pratt, C. 1948. *I learn from children.* New York: Simon and Schuster.

Pratt, C. 1973. The play school. In *Experimental schools revisited,* ed. C. Winsor. New York: Agathon.

Winsor, C., ed. 1973. *Experimental schools revisited.* New York: Agathon.

2

The Art of Block Building

Harriet M. Johnson

Introduction

What are blocks for?

Toy makers have put blocks on the market for many long years, decorating them with letters of the alphabet in an attempt to sneak something "useful" into a child's play. But young children usually ignored the letters and piled the blocks into gay towers. Then, some 30 or more years ago, school people began to take children's play seriously, to say that play itself was educational, and a different kind of blocks came on the market. They were just pieces of unpainted wood, the same width and thickness, and with lengths twice or four times as great as the unit block. A few curves, cylinders, and half-thickness blocks were added, but all with lengths that fitted into the measurements of the basic blocks. These blocks, devised by Caroline Pratt, founder of the City and Country School, were in use in the nursery, now called Harriet Johnson Nursery School, which Harriet Johnson directed from its organization in 1914 until her death.

Many schools for young children now use these blocks. They have been found to be the most useful tool for self-education that young children can play with and work with. Most teachers have concentrated on the value of these blocks as giving children an opportunity to reproduce their experiences quickly and then play them out actively with their block creations. Harriet Johnson was well aware of this value and has written about the use of blocks in Children in the Nursery School *([1928] 1972).*

The present Bank Street College of Education was founded by Lucy Sprague Mitchell in 1916 as the Bureau of Educational Experiments. In 1919 a nursery school was added to the bureau's work, and in 1930 the Cooperative School for Student Teachers (later known as the Cooperative School for Teachers) was established. One part of the Cooperative School's work was disseminating the experimental work of the bureau through publication of "The Cooperating School Pamphlets."

The first pamphlet was Harriet M. Johnson's *The Art of Block Building*, published in 1933 by the John Day Company in New York. Other pamphlets proposed for the series were Barbara Biber's *Children's Drawings* and Lucy Sprague Mitchell's *Young Geographers*. The editors for this series were Lucy Sprague Mitchell, Harriet M. Johnson, Jessie Stanton, and Ellen Steele. This chapter is based on Bank Street College of Education Publications' 1966 reprint of *The Art of Block Building*.

In the present study, however, Harriet Johnson has concentrated on another value of the blocks, a value often overlooked. These blocks in the creative hands of children also become an art medium. Grown-ups are still prone to organize a curriculum for one area of learning and then another, and to work out equipment that they think will develop one patch of a child and then another. But children just refuse to respond in this piecemeal fashion. They remain consistently whole people, reacting to situations with all their lively interests mixed together. They are small scientists eagerly investigating the world that they can lay their hands on; small human beings interested in other human beings; dramatists playing out their experiences, modifying them to give themselves a strategic position in the world of grown-ups; workmen exulting in their techniques; artists enjoying design and pattern-form, balance in size and color, repetition. The wonder of blocks is the many-sided constructive experiences they yield to the many-sided constructive child—and every child is such if guided by a many-sided constructive parent or teacher.

Harriet Johnson was such a teacher. She watched the young children in her nursery school with a scientist's eye and recorded with a scientist's accuracy. She appreciated keenly the beauty of these children's creations, as well as the thinking and social interactions and workmanship they involved. Thus she came to write The Art of Block Building (1933). Here she has separated from the many-sided experiences children live through in their block building the elusive element that we call "art," a precious element seldom lacking in children's work, but, alas, seldom recognized by teachers or parents whose eyes are so earnestly fixed on "bringing up a child right" that they fail to enjoy children and their art.

—Lucy Sprague Mitchell
April 1945

*   *   *

In the school of which I am writing, (which was called the Nursery School of the Bureau of Educational Experiments, later called the Harriet Johnson Nursery School, and now named Bank Street School for Children) and in others with which I am familiar, block building is one of the major interests. A description of the activities of these schools or a discussion of their curricula would show constructive play with blocks as a central and coordinating feature of their programs.

As I have watched block building over a period of years, the method by which children develop techniques in construction and the versatility they show in their use of blocks have been of increasing interest to me. Still more absorbing has been the realization that almost inevitably, in the block building history of group after group, there appear art forms, comparable in spirit to those produced by older children with plastic materials such as paints or clay.

I have tried to present in these pages the use of blocks as a medium of expression and to give a glimpse of the ideas and feelings expressed by children from 2 to 6 years of age.

The first use of blocks among young children is not properly building. Blocks are carried from place to place, or they may be stacked or massed in irregular, conglomerate piles before the period of construction begins. During this time, children are probably getting an experience no less real than their later one when adults can recognize the result as illustrating actual problems in balance, construction, design, or representation. The early experience holds value because of the chance to gain acquaintance with this particular building tool by manipulation and by using various forms and various spaces.

Between 2 and 3 years of age, real construction begins and has been found to follow broadly three or four lines of development, especially in regard to the techniques. Blocks in these early years are comparable to such plastic materials as crayons, paint, or clay, and their use is dependent upon impulse, which is influencing the young builder.

The blocks in use in the indoor playrooms are shown here (Figure 1). These blocks were designed by Caroline Pratt and have always been used in the City and Country School. She has never given them her name and so they are found on the market under the name of the manufacturer and under various trade

names. It will be seen that all the other forms can be made from the unit by multiplication or division, except the cylinders or curves. The cylinders conform in height to the unit and posts. The curves are of similar width and thickness. In addition to the other forms, small colored cubes one-inch square are used.

It is essential that the blocks be cut very accurately so that all edges are even and that the multiples and divisions of the unit are exact, because they are tools for the children's use, and the most desirable building habits will be established only if the materials are stable and precise.

Occasionally the illustrations show blocks other than those in the set described. This occurs only in the youngest groups where a wider variety of materials is provided.

The sketches of actual constructions made by the children are taken from the daily records of teachers and students. They are accurate in the kind and number of blocks used, but because they were made hastily and because few of us are skilled in drafting, they are far from accurate in perspective and proportion. They are not drawn to the same scale, because they were designed only as a graphic record of the day's building activity.

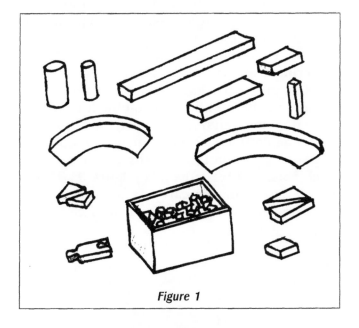

Figure 1

The blocks and accessories in the set above were those used at Bank Street by Harriet Johnson. Sets vary in types of blocks and accessories, depending on the manufacturer, but all blocks are based on the following proportions—1:2:4 (half as high are they are wide; twice as long as they are wide).

Repetition, the tower, and the row

All parents and teachers will agree that repetition in one form or another is characteristic of children who are just beginning to perfect their locomotion or their language. They climb up steps only to descend and climb again. They throw a ball only to retrieve it and throw again, unless they can induce an adult to take one step in the repetitive process. After they learn to say "I slide down" or "Want see," adults turn gray as the refrain beats on their tired ears.

It has been very interesting to us to find repetition in many forms appearing again and again as the first constructive use of blocks.

A child can repeat by piling blocks one on top of another. At first, the resulting tower may be an irregular one, threatening to fall as each additional block is placed. At this stage, lofty towers are not found in the records, because they crash before a sketch can be made of them.

Early differences in personality traits are plainly shown here. There are children who, from the first, attempt to straighten their block edges and who do not try for perilous heights, seemingly able to judge when the last steady block is in place. There are others who fling their blocks together, not concerned with the perfection or the stability of the structure.

Whichever method individual children choose, the general tendency toward repetition is universal. Among the youngest children, it almost seems as if their object is to clear all shelves, so persistently do they add another and another and another block to a tower or a row, or as will be seen, repeat a pattern over and over again.

Edith, who had discovered that blocks were not just luggage but building material, achieved this tower—first one block and then another, laid as nearly as possible in the same place (Figure 2).

None of the methods in use among young builders is superseded entirely by new and elaborate building techniques. Rather each form evolves into more and more detailed

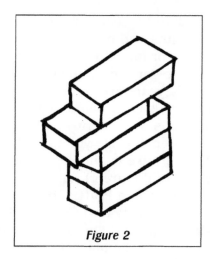

Figure 2

constructions, which are more and more difficult to execute as skill of hand and an understanding of the possibilities within the material develop.

At first the evolution takes the form of experimenting within the chosen plan. Having made a pile of blocks, perhaps all of one kind, builders vary the kind or combine kinds or they do stunt building, balancing large blocks on a smaller base or on a narrow support.

Danny placed a tower of three cubes on each corner of his cube box (Figure 3). This was a task requiring care and delicacy of handling as he began on the nearer corners

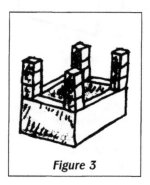

Figure 3

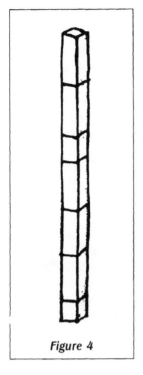

Figure 4

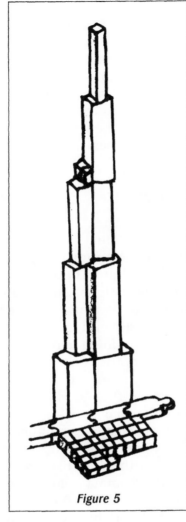

Figure 5

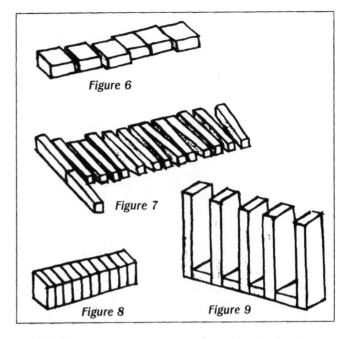

Figure 6

Figure 7

Figure 8

Figure 9

and reached across the first towers to place blocks on the farther ones.

Sasha tried repeating balancing stunts with units and half units (Figure 4). While placing the two top blocks, she steadied those below with her left hand.

Henry took blocks of various sizes to make his tower (Figure 5). The trains and the flooring of cubes seemed to be accessories.

With the data on hand, it is impossible to tell whether or not the tower is an earlier pattern than the row. Traditional influences, as well as modern tendencies, are at work toward establishing an interest in height. Also, to lay one block upon another may be a simpler process than to place one next to another in a line. The examples given here of the tower and the row were made within the same month. The recipe is similar: first one block and then another is placed in serial order on the floor.

Later, when less hampered by the difficulties of mere manipulation of the material, children embroider the pattern in a variety of ways. Instead of laying the blocks closely side by side or edge to edge, they may space them, alternating the sizes as they place them or alternating single blocks with low tiers.

Repetition follows a syncopated rhythm in Danny and Henry's building (Figures 6, 7, 8, 9).

13

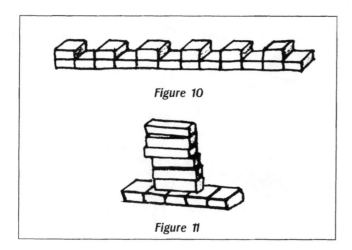

Figure 10

Figure 11

nique and a detail in larger architectural planning. It is almost as if the first year of building were a practice period which is to lay the foundations for the more technical work of the advanced student.

Beneath all the examples given and illustrated runs the youthful pattern: put down one, and then another, and then another, and then another.

Bridging

After a time, given these architecturally exact building materials, certain problems in construction invariably seem to arise. By this I mean that although no patterns are set and no suggestions are made by the teachers, the constructions made increase in elaboration and in difficulty, and fairly predictable stages in the building activities can be observed.

These two patterns (Figures 10, 11), the tower and the row, are preeminently characteristic of youthful building. Sometimes, towers and rows are combined.

When children can make single towers with blocks on edge as well as flat on their faces or with combinations of sizes or shapes, they find that a series of towers makes a wall, just as a series of rows makes a floor (Figure 12).

At first, handling blocks, then arranging them in towers and rows, or walls and flooring, absorbs children. Interest in these types of construction in and of themselves is short-lived, because they are soon incorporated into more elaborate constructions. They are no longer valued as an end, but only as a tech-

One of the early problems is that of bridging, of setting up two blocks, leaving a space between them and roofing that space with another block.

It is sometimes a difficult problem to place the uprights at an appropriate distance apart, so that the third block will bridge the space. An acute dilemma occurs when one of the longest blocks on the shelves is laid flat, and another is placed upright at each end of it. Such a problem has been known to block some children completely, and the younger child is usually defeated at the first failure.

Edith twice set up the figure sketched, all three blocks double units, and tried to bridge the space with a double (Figure 13).

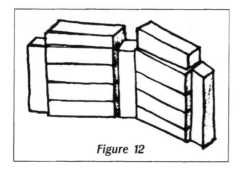

Figure 12

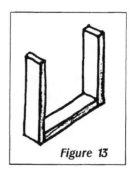

Figure 13

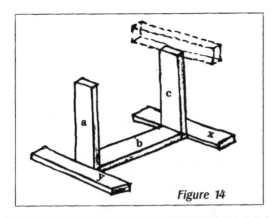

Figure 14

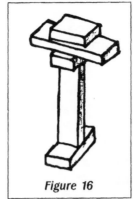

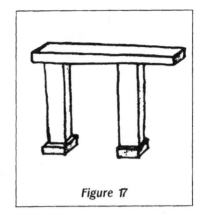

Figure 16

Figure 17

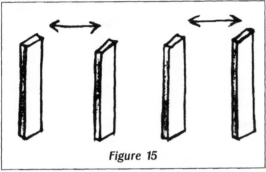

Figure 15

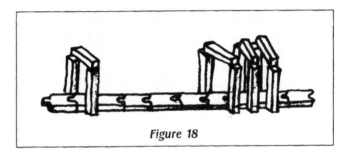

Figure 18

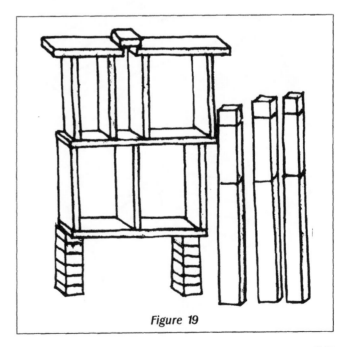

Figure 19

She then set up *a*, *b*, and *c* (doubles) and tried to bridge them as usual with another double. When she found that it would not fit, she tried it across *c* (dotted lines), then laid it in position *x*, and added *y* (Figure 14).

Danny spaced four double units on end, but did no more about it (Figure 15). He approached success here, though his bridge did not yet span a space between two uprights (Figure 16).

This was followed by achieving the bridge technique (Figure 17).

Repetition takes possession of the young builder as soon as the new technique is established (Figure 18).

Facility leads to a combination of styles and methods. The tower and the bridge form "a high building" with "fire ladders" at the side. Sasha built as shown (Figure 19), then propped the three uprights against the "high building." She showed elation when the feat was accomplished, jumping and clapping her hands and smiling broadly.

Enclosures

Enclosures appear early in the building activities. To put four blocks together so that a space is completely enclosed is not a simple task. However it appears, and once learned, repetitive enclosures seem to be the next step. That is, every new device, idea, method, or pattern lends itself to the repetitive formula.

Sarah worked for a full month before she succeeded in placing the last block which completely enclosed a space (Figures 20, 21). The driving force was her own initiative.

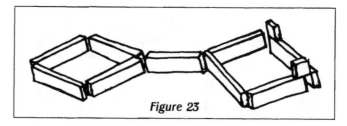

Figure 23

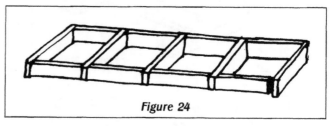

Figure 24

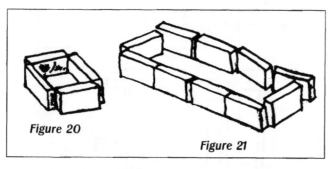

Figure 20

Figure 21

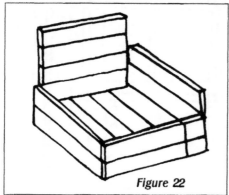

Figure 22

Sarah later built double units and two half units as shown (Figure 22)—a marked elaboration of her first attempt.

Fancy free, now that skill of hand had been acquired, Sarah arranged her enclosures in patterned, repetitive form (Figure 23).

Danny arranged a row of four enclosures (Figure 24). Repetition takes the field.

This time, he set his enclosures on end—or are they a series of bridges?—first one, and then another, and then another (Figure 25).

Michael varied the square design (Figure 26).

Here are enclosures repeated and elaborated. Michael set double units on edges, making a most pleasing pattern (Figure 27). He began with the pentagon, then added the triangle. He did not achieve the square and triangle at the first placing of the blocks, but pushed them about. He said, "Pushing them in" once as he worked, but was not heard to name his building.

Let no academic adult here raise the question: "Do you call children's attention to the shapes they have made, the rectangle, the triangle, the pentagon, and give them their names?" The

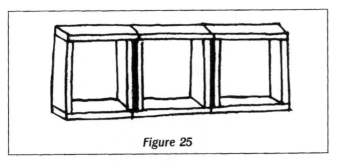

Figure 25

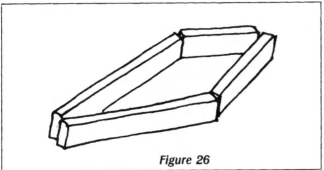

Figure 26

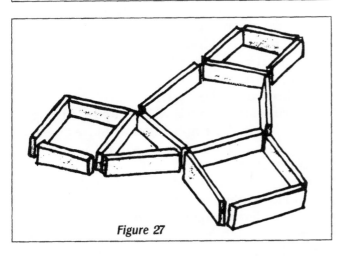

Figure 27

the quality of plasticity and almost of malleability. It will yield to the child's desire. Children are absorbed, intent, and satisfied during this process, as anyone who has watched a block building period can testify. Information is completely irrelevant here. It would remain irrelevant even if we granted that the subject was one suited to the preschool ages.

Michael, still intent upon odd-shaped enclosures, builds what he calls "the wow wow circle" (Figure 28).

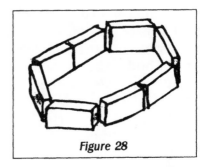

Figure 28

Enclosures become more elaborate. This (Figure 29) was called "a house," and dolls were placed in each section.

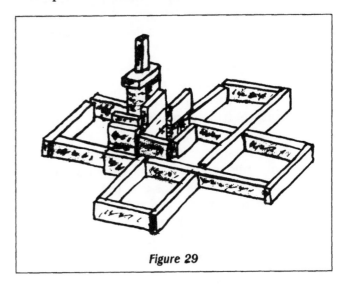

Figure 29

experience which building holds for children is varied, to be sure, but it is useless unless it springs from some impulse within them. At this stage, they are wrestling with the problem of making material (which to the uninformed adult may seem factual and unyielding) take on

When children are once able to see blocks as building material that is capable of being put together in an ordered arrangement, a variety of methods, patterns, and techniques seem to suggest themselves to them. With age, there is a steady increase in facility, imagination, elaboration of design, and actual number of blocks used.

Patterns

As soon as children begin to acquire facility in the use of blocks, so that they feel at home with the material, another tendency appears, namely that of building in balanced and decorative patterns. We have been led to the conclusion that blocks are essentially the most admirable plastic material for young children, because with blocks they seem able to arrange, to design, to compose.

I do not wish to imply that children say, even to themselves, "Now I will make a design," but that with child after child in a group, with child after child of age after age, unnamed and unused buildings appear, delightful to the adult eye in the rhythm of their balance and the originality of their design and decoration.

In such decorative buildings are incorporated any or all of the building principles described, and with them, the repetitive impulse finds full scope; in fact, repetition is one of the features of design.

Again, it must be said that no patterns are set for the children, that no comments are made upon their buildings except in the way of general response to a given child's explanation or remark. Occasionally, children are asked, "Would you like to build?" or they are told that they may use any kind of block if they seem to

be inclined to restrict themselves to one size. In the beginning of the school year, the children are shown the blocks and are told that they may build. The only restriction placed upon the use of the materials is that they are not to be thrown and that structures are not to be knocked down. Probably the most potent factor in establishing a creative use of blocks is the genuine interest of the teachers in block building as an expressive art—an outlet for the manifold experiences through which children are living, whether they are the intentional experiences of the school or those that life itself thrusts upon them. In children's reaction to their "work," the teachers see such evidences of interest, absorption, and elation that their enthusiasm is kindled.

When a child who has not had the experience with block building comes into a group at 4 or 5 years of age, that child seems to follow much the same order of development that younger children do, but of course passes through the various phases at a much more rapid rate of speed. The steps or stages that have been described seem invariably to appear first. The rate at which children pass through these stages, the emphasis they place on each, and the lines of development that they subsequently follow vary with the individual.

The inclination to seek a patterned arrangement also varies, but only, I think, in degree. There are few young builders who seem to lack a feeling for pattern and balance. For the most part, the design they follow is more or less evenly balanced, almost a formal one. Often the rhythm is a muscular one; that is, the child places a block at the right, then at the left, or a block at the front of a construction, then at the back. The fact that opposite sides of a large construction are in absolute balance, even when the design is intricate, seems to suggest that the builder is dominated by an image, whether kinesthetic or visual, we do not know.

However, younger children, having completed structures that in the opinion of adults are quite perfect, often massed blocks all about and concealed the patterns entirely in conglomerate piles, as if they either did not see the patterns or did not value them.

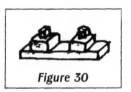

Figure 30

Just why did Edith choose from the block shelves this varied combination (Figure 30)? Both cubes set on top were yellow.

At the same age, she made this very similar pattern, but here she has taken length for her accent and has placed posts—evenly spaced—on each of the double units (Figure 31).

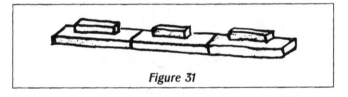

Figure 31

Danny, still very much in the stage of stacking, made this very unusual arrangement of posts (Figure 32). More were laid than sketched here. In spite of its being a rather tricky pattern of follow consistently, the alternation was maintained.

How can a child who has worked so little with this material, who is so immature in other details of development, in language, and indeed in block building, keep consistently in mind this sort of alternation? The answer is probably that he did not keep it in mind but in muscle, or at least that it was feeling, not thinking, that guided him.

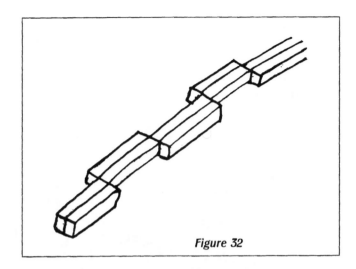

Figure 32

Sometimes the pattern is a small one, repeated again and again. Sarah used posts as illustrated (Figure 33).

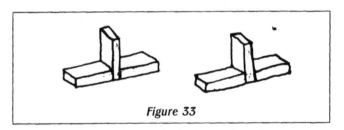

Figure 33

Figure 34

This design (Figure 34) in layers, small cubes tucked between rows of larger blocks, appears frequently. Tony did not name his construction.

Spreading, flat buildings were characteristic of Tony. The conventional balance does not possess him as it seems to possess some children, but to the adult onlooker the design element has charm.

At this age, naming may be a part of building, so this (Figure 35) is a "Big, long, long train."

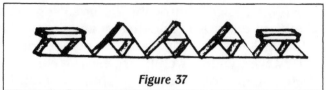

Figure 37

Rather difficult task this was, to balance long blocks on their edges and to place the upright unit with its triangle cap at a point where it can hold the balance (Figure 38).

Judith was a child aware of an intention, for she called this (Figure 39) "decoration."

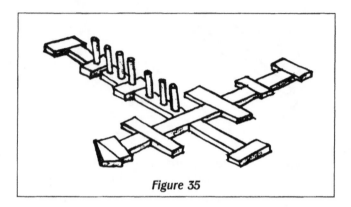

Figure 35

This building (Figure 36) which Tony made 4 months later was unnamed. It illustrates the way structures become more intricate as children grow older.

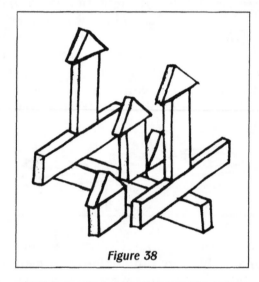

Figure 38

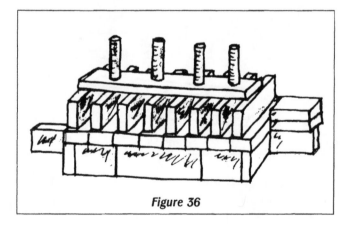

Figure 36

One feels a lovely balance in Ingrid's building (Figure 37). She made just this, then left it. She did not name it.

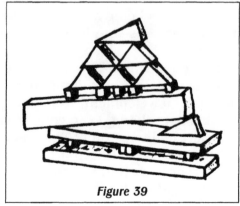

Figure 39

Representation

Somewhere along in the early block building history, an impulse to name arises. This does not mean that the buildings resemble the things they are called. Children may give names to their constructions, or their drawings, because of the example of older children who do so with intention, or, more probably, because of injudicious adult questioning. Teachers are quite careful to avoid suggesting, even by questions, that children name their buildings, because they have learned that real representative building comes at a later stage.

Among 2- and 3-year-old children, we find naming, but very rarely play use of the structures made with small indoor blocks. Naming becomes very usual among older children. The name is often announced as an advance plan. Dramatic use of buildings increases as the techniques of building are well learned, so that the material is no longer master of the situation as it is earlier.

At later ages, the dramatic impulse is so strong that the buildings reproduce or symbolize actual structures or experiences that the children are recalling and serve as stage settings. A group of children build a railway system, tracks, stations, switching engines, a tower for the signal attendant, and even the building to which the railroad employees go to get their watches tested. These standpatter (dolls made of copper wire, with weighted feet and wooden beads for heads and hands) employees took their meals on a roof garden constructed by one of the girls in the group. All the buildings in this play scheme were built by individuals, but the play with them afterward was cooperative and interrelated. Play of this sort represents a fairly mature understanding.

Other materials, like crayons and clay, are more freely in use and serve as supplements to the play or as elaborations of it. Tools have been introduced so that bench products can be made and added to the scheme of play of which the block building is the center.

With all the opportunities for elaboration of the representative structures, we find some surprising, though probably logical, developments. In the first place, we realize as we look at the block buildings that repetition continues to be much in evidence. The tower has grown more complicated, but its construction still means placing first one block and then another in a pile of sorts. The pile may be foursquare, made of repeated bridge units superimposed one upon another, or it may be an enclosure of solid walls. Children call upon all the techniques they acquired in their early experimenting period, combining the simple patterns, including many in a single structure, and using many more blocks in the process. Secondly, with the increasing tendency of children to give names to their structures, we find the design elements persisting and becoming more intricate and, at the same time, taking on attributes that we usually associate with symbolism as we know it in the artistic sense.

Figure 40

Henry's building (Figure 40) strikes a commonly accepted pattern in general movement, the larger base narrowing to the slender, terminal tower, quite in unrecognized acceptance of New York's set-back fashion.

Henry's name for his tower, "a park," may have meant that he had observed buildings in a park or, more probably, it may have been an overflow from his awakening social and language interest. That he also mentioned bridges, smokestacks, and doors to the entranced Joan (who listened, watched, and tried to direct him) suggests that his language was not closely related to his building. The three small blocks at the tip of the tower were called "lights."

Andrea's "Empire State" is an illustration of a very practical cob house construction with very little elaboration (Figure 41). Its name is almost inevitable, because Manhattan is dominated by that vertiginous piece of architecture.

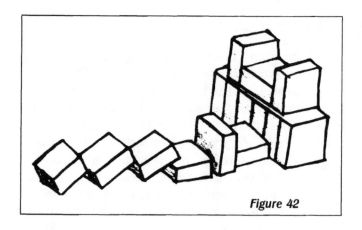

Figure 42

Figure 41

Betty came through with a statement: "A house and these are the stairs" (Figure 42).

Do children see stairs in some such pattern or are they unable to grasp the technique of making gradually decreasing piles, set side by side? Because they can build a train shed completely enclosed, so that no train can enter

or leave it, because they make a highchair for the baby taller than the house in which it is to be placed, because the early drawing of a boat may be a collection of smokestacks and funnels, we know that the young hand needs much practice and that though the young mind can assimilate certain outstanding features, it does not take in a total complicated conception.

At a later age, Andrea was quite capable of using stairs as a part of a beautifully balanced building (Figure 43), and of arranging doll blankets on them as carpets.

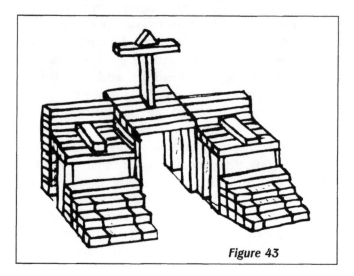

Figure 43

22

The really dramatic quality about these young builders is not their mastery of techniques but their attitude toward the material. It is essentially that of the artist. Even when they do representative building, it is the essence, not the bald form, that they make alive. We adults are prosaic in the use of our skills. We learn to speak or to write, and thereafter practice these arts in a strictly utilitarian and unimaginative fashion. It is a rare person whose speech is marked by originality or whose thoughts find expression in written language that seems really her or his own—that has the quality of the individual producing it.

Children speak with blocks. They say in their own way what they have to say. It may be fanciful or humorous. They may express a resemblance or a parallel in their building, or a symbol may stand for a complex conception.

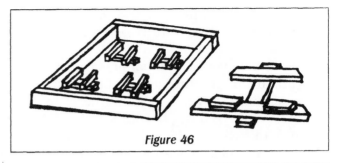

Figure 46

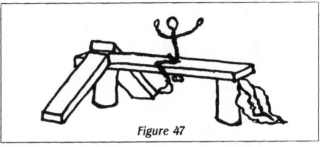

Figure 47

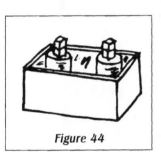

Figure 44

Jeanne sees her two cylinders as "candlesticks," and so do we (Figure 44).

"The river, that goes up and down like waves," was as effective to Jan as an inspired simile to an older poet (Figure 45).

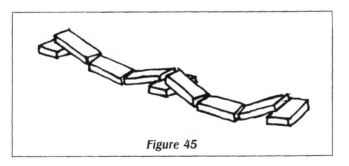

Figure 45

Edward makes a fleet or a litter of "baby airplanes with the mama plane" (Figure 46).

Jackie's "horse with me on it" is an example of how little the limitations of the material need cramp a child (Figure 47).

Richard's "Empire State" is "like the real one, big at the bottom and then smaller" (Figure 48).

John and Lucio saw these blocks, set up on their ends, with imaginative eyes. It is "a parade"—not quite so orderly as some

Figure 48

(Figure 49). Perhaps the crowd is gathered to welcome a visiting celebrity. Even the airplanes are here.

Judith has used a wide variety of material in her unnamed structure (Figure 50). Its balance is not entirely conventional, and therefore perhaps more pleasing to adults.

Norman's "hospital," in its arrangement of planes and lines, has a modern flavor startling to adults (Figure 51). We cannot know what it meant to him—not an experiment in planes, we may be sure, but some sort of an affective experience was his as he worked, absorbed, sober, intent, oblivious of the other builders until the last zigzag block was laid and his work was finished.

Joan's unnamed structure shows some outstanding features in balance (Figure 52).

Figure 50

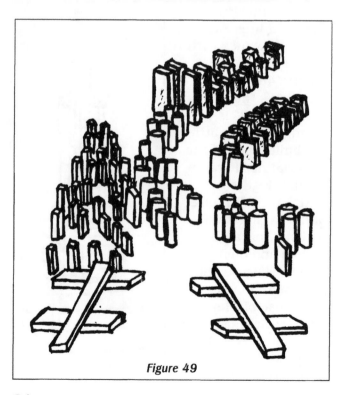

Figure 49

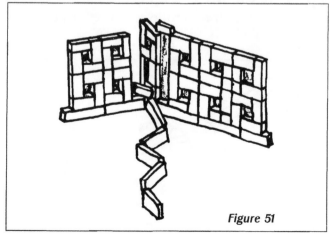

Figure 51

24

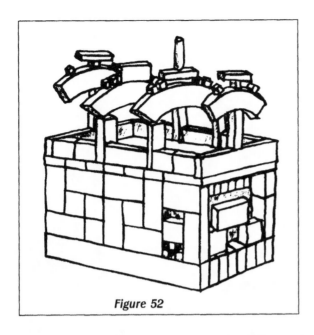

Figure 52

She has matched the cubes in colors from the right to the left side. She has let in three windows in each of her side walls. Two of them are made after the classic design favored by older builders. In these, the opening will just take a half-unit block. Put in place, it closes the window, as can be seen. The third window on either side has a slightly different construction, making a larger opening. She has apparently raised the sash, holding it up with an arrangement of three cubes. The opposite side of this structure is identical to the one sketched. And so it goes.

The difficulty in gathering these examples from our records has been in deciding which among many to include. Many of the most intricate and enchanting constructions were too elaborate for the lay hand to sketch.

For the most part, I have emphasized what I have called the use of blocks as art material, rather than their use in dramatic reproduction—the play with form and balance in their use, rather than with representation and utility.

We have not realized sufficiently the richness of this kind of play material on the one hand, nor the richness of children's imaginative resources on the other. No adult could have planned a didactic method that could have stimulated children to this sort of activity, but also no such building is found unless favorable conditions are made for it. These include a lavish supply of materials and a program that gives to children firsthand experiences which make them more aware of the world and their place in it. Added to this is an attitude on the part of the teacher that the interest of children in construction is significant and must be protected. A teacher will feel a genuine enthusiasm for the block building program after she or he has watched such development as the preceding material would indicate.

The details of the teaching techniques that help develop profitable use of blocks cannot be discussed here, but the essentials are a recognition of the possibilities in block building, actual respect for and interest in the activity, the provision of space and time for it, and the protection of the children from interruption and encroachment from less interested individuals. Given such conditions and such a teacher attitude, I believe that in any group of healthy children, the progressive development of structures such as these will be found.

References

Johnson, H. [1933] 1966. *The art of block building.* New York: Bank Street College of Education.

Johnson, H. [1928] 1972. *Children in the nursery school.* New York: Agathon. Reissued with an introductory essay by Barbara Biber.

3

Children Learn about Science through Block Building

Mary W. Moffitt

Adults who look upon block building as an idle pastime or a childish activity often fail to realize that block building is a lifetime activity. Whether one is an architect planning a building, a delivery person loading a truck, or a homemaker storing groceries in a cupboard, each is handling various units or forms that fit together in different spatial relations and are influenced by balance and stability. So it is for children as they build with blocks.

It is somewhat difficult to isolate science content in block building without overlapping into other content areas, such as mathematics and geography. Size, shape, area, and volume are related to both scientific and mathematical concepts. When children build a structure or represent the world symbolically with houses, bridges, ramps, and tunnels, they are dealing with geographical concepts, as well as with scientific concepts of space, distance, direction, grids, patterns, and mapping.

Meeting the goals of science education

Perhaps it is easier to think about block building as an activity that meets many of the present goals for science education. We are beginning to realize that science content is better learned through the development of the processes of inquiry, such as observing, comparing, classifying, predicting, and interpreting. Block building is a medium that is particularly well adapted for children to use these processes. Children's scientific thinking is stimulated as they discover and invent new forms, compare and classify different sizes and shapes, test ideas of "What will happen if . . . ?," or learn to use clues to predict outcomes because they have become familiar with the properties of the blocks with which they build.

Learning the properties of blocks

Science education today emphasizes the importance for young children of learning about the properties of matter, and in block building children learn about properties of

Scientific thinking requires regular patterns of thought, and block building stimulates children to develop various ways of systematizing their constructions.

different kinds of blocks. Each block has physical qualities, such as size, shape, weight, and three-dimensionality; it has properties of thickness, width, and length. Children soon learn to differentiate these dimensions as they use the blocks in their structures. A block may be seen as similar or dissimilar to another block, depending on how it is to be used in positional relationships with other blocks.

Children learn also that a block may be placed flat, on edge, or on end, and the use of these surfaces may be combined to create different characteristics in their structures.

Weight is a factor in learning about size, because larger unit blocks are heavier than smaller ones. The way children grasp a block elicits tactile interpretations of weight, sometimes misleading ones, until children learn to grasp the block differently. For instance, if children grasp the end of a block that is a foot or more long, they may think that the block is heavier than when they grasp it in the center, where it is better balanced; thus the hand is a fulcrum and the block is a lever. Many other properties of the blocks—such as the curvature or angularity, edges, corners, and surface—can be seen and felt as the child handles different shapes.

When children become aware of the similarities and dissimilarities in the size and shape of various blocks, they tend to match and sort them accordingly. This activity is a form of classification that is important for scientific thinking. Encouraging children to put away blocks according to different features enhances the classification process.

Seeing a block structure as a system

Two major conceptual ideas stressed in science education are those of *systems* and the *interactions* that occur within systems. A block construction is a system composed of parts that are in equilibrium, and this system is established through the interaction of certain parts that are in balance.

Scientific thinking requires regular patterns of thought, and block building stimulates children to develop various ways of systematizing their constructions. As children build they learn that there are certain sequential patterns that they must follow when they place different blocks in relationship to one another. Children tend to develop a variety of sequential patterns, which they repeat over and over again. Watch how children establish a pattern as they build. If a child lays two blocks parallel, she may lay two blocks parallel on top of them but in an opposite direction. Or she may set up two blocks and then bridge them and continue the pattern to develop a vertical system. Through the production and reproduction of these and many other patterns, a child begins to grasp a concept of the whole-part relationship within her structure or system.

Reversibility is the beginning of logical thinking, according to Piaget (1963). A way to observe children's ability to perceive the reverse of their sequential patterns is to suggest that they take down their structure in reverse order of their putting it up. You may suggest, "Can you take your building down

Children learn to work with a cause-and-effect approach and to predict the stress and strain resulting from the forces of gravity interacting on various parts of their buildings.

without it falling down?" and note the child's awareness of reversibility as he removes the appropriate blocks in reverse order.

Learning about interaction of forces within a system

Equilibrium, balance, and stability are governed by the pull of gravity. When children first start building, they are likely to place blocks on top of one another in haphazard fashion, and, of course, the tower soon tumbles over. Watch for the time when children begin to place the blocks in more careful alignment or when they straighten the sides of the tower with their hands. These actions indicate that the children are aware that some action is necessary if they want to build higher, although they don't understand the concept of center of gravity as a force that is interacting among the blocks of their structure. But children learn quickly to predict when a tower has reached the height at which it becomes unsteady. They learn to look for certain clues to the tower's stability, and they indicate their awareness by the way they place each additional block or by the way they often extend their fingers in anticipation of the moment of collapse. Children's perception of stability also can be seen when they test their structure by placing a block gingerly or by placing it tentatively and then quickly taking it away because they perceive that the structure has reached maximum stability.

With experience, children become adept in adapting to gravitational forces in different ways for effective building.

Although balance and stability are obtained at first through trial and error, with experience children become quite adept in adapting to gravitational forces in different ways for effective building. They learn where to place a block so that it will support another block, or they learn the necessity of moving a block slightly to obtain better balance. Gradually children perceive, too, that a broader base will provide greater stability when they wish to build higher.

Children learn to deal with disequilibrium through the use of counterbalancing. They do this in different ways. Sometimes they achieve balance by interlocking the faces of the different blocks. Or they learn to use more blocks (more weight) to counterbalance a block, depending on how it is supported.

Many children have a tendency to seek right and left balance as they design their buildings. If they place a block on one side of the structure, they often place a similar block in a similar position on the other side of the structure. To selectively place objects in this way, a child must have developed perception of pattern and ready identification of form similarities.

Children, like scientists, focus their attention on the problems of stability and seek ways to build that are successful and satisfying to them. Much stimulation to thinking comes from working out problems that arise from the interaction of forces related to balance and equilibrium. "How may I build higher?" "How will this block fit here?" "What must I do to keep it from falling over?"

Accumulation of experience in building all kinds of structures provides a child with a good idea of what can or cannot be done with the material. A child learns to work with a cause-and-effect approach and to predict the structural stress resulting from the forces of gravity interacting on various parts of a building.

Learning about space

A block is a form that takes up space either (primarily) vertically or horizontally, depending on how it is placed. When children build by placing one block upon another, they soon realize that the structure becomes taller. Likewise, a long structure results when blocks are placed end to end in a continuous pattern across the floor. This pattern may continue until limitation is reached in the form of a wall or some other object. Then there must be a change of direction if the pattern is to continue.

Bridging space is a problem requiring perception of the space between two or more blocks. A child must select an appropriate-size block to fit the space between the blocks, or make an adjustment to accommodate the particular block being used to span the space.

Space may be enclosed in different ways, and smaller enclosures may be made within larger enclosures. Children like to put objects in these various-size enclosures, but they have to learn that what is put into an enclosure must be in ratio to the enclosed space—

Bridging space is a problem requiring perception of space between two or more blocks.

in other words, it cannot be bigger than the area enclosed. Similar problems occur when children wish to push a toy truck or boat under a bridge or through a tunnel. They must perceive that the object must be in ratio to the defined space under the bridge or within the tunnel.

As children build, their structures take up more and more space. Sometimes they have to change direction or change the pattern because of limitations in surface area. Some children tend to build very compactly, while others tend to extend their structures in multiple directions. Some children enjoy exploring vertical space and want to build high. Teachers sometimes become fearful and caution the children not to extend their structure beyond their own height. Once children have developed some construction skills, however, this limitation curtails the activity and the opportunity to deal with problems that are encountered in building to greater heights.

Through construction and dramatic play, children learn that there are certain conditions and limitations in space. Children who have extensive experiences with block building soon acquire perceptive judgment in dealing with space, and they build accordingly. They become aware of the need for caution when a building seems unsteady, and they perceive when a change of direction is needed. Such children also seem to exhibit a well-defined sense of self in space, and they can move around delicately balanced structures without knocking them down. The children seem to become sensitized in how to move and how to handle the material with ease and self-assurance.

Comparing dimensions by measuring

Many opportunities for comparing length, height, and depth are inherent in block building. Each block may be used as a unit of measurement, and children discover equivalency among the different-size units. Thus they are able to substitute a large unit for several smaller units or vice versa.

When a child builds vertically or horizontally, a rope or string may be used to measure the height or length of the construction. The rope, in turn, becomes a unit of measurement that may be used to compare the block structure to the length and height of other objects in the room. The teacher may indicate, "Your building is as long as my desk" or ". . . as high as the chalkboard."

A child also may measure depth when she builds a high enclosure: "How deep is it?" If the enclosure is large enough, sometimes children like to get into it. They use their bodies as the unit of measurement and may find out, for instance, that the enclosure is as deep as they are tall.

Building architectural forms

Block structures readily become architectural forms. Children create tunnels, bridges, ramps, and towers as they organize the blocks into certain positional relationships. The builder soon learns to use the blocks to make different forms in a miniaturized world in which she can use toy cars, trucks, and the like. In developing architectural forms the child learns to deal with problems of proximity and the relationship of one type of structure to another. Various kinds of buildings assume the approximation of distance and direction in mapping out the reproduction of the larger world. Roadways have direction and are in certain positional relationship to bridges or tunnels. Buildings have certain relationships to roads and other kinds of buildings. Some buildings have distinctive characteristics that children attempt to reproduce, such as garages, houses, and stores.

A ramp is an inclined plane, but it can also be a device for raising objects from one level to another with a minimum of effort. Children learn the function of the inclined plane when they place a ramp for a roadway or some place of entry for their toys. A child tests the ramp's function by pushing the toy up the slope or by letting the toy roll freely down the ramp.

Thinking creatively and scientifically

Invention and discovery are part of scientific thinking. A successful scientist has a creative mind and creates new forms by finding new relationships among established ideas.

In block building the material is fluid, providing infinite possibilities for a child to develop ideas and improvise or create at will—provided, of course, that the child has an adequate number of blocks with which to work and the opportunities to use them.

Developing the skills of inquiry through block building seems to be a realistic approach to science content. Usually young children tend to work intuitively rather than logically. It is best to permit children to invent explanations for their experiences as they deal with the concrete materials and manipulate them in different ways. Through exploration,

invention, and discovery, children develop ways of thinking about physical phenomena that they encounter in their construction. In this way they build knowledge that will be relative to more complex concepts later on. Too often children are urged to deal with abstract ideas before they are prepared to do so. All that this effort accomplishes is children being able to mouth the words without understanding them.

Teachers should not attempt to teach science content formally; rather, they should reinforce what the child has done by making a descriptive comment, such as, "You have learned how to balance that long block with some smaller ones" or "You have found the right-size truck to go through your tunnel."

Asking questions judiciously is another way to help children focus on an aspect of their work—for example, "Can you make a ramp for the cars to go into your garage?" or "Where will you put the road?"

It is advisable from time to time to get children to verbalize how they solved a problem in construction by asking, "How did you get those blocks to balance?" or "How did you know where to put the big block?"

Inquiry-centered learning allows children to develop their thinking and can lead learners to discover for themselves what they are ready to understand. It is important, however, for teachers to develop insight into how these processes function for scientific thinking. Furthermore, to be effective a teacher must be a communicator in these processes when working with children.

Reference

Piaget, J. 1963. *The psychology of intelligence.* Patterson, NJ: Littlefield Adams.

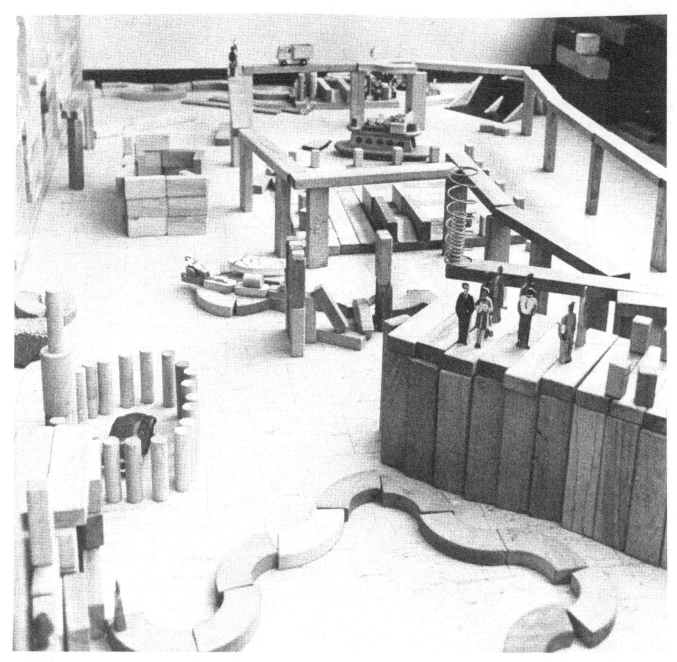

In developing architectural forms the child learns to deal with problems of proximity and the relationship of one type of structure to another.

34

4

The Block Builder Mathematician

Kristina Leeb-Lundberg

A child's artistry in—and feeling for—block building is closely related to the true mathematician's view of mathematics as a creative art. The aesthetic pleasure that adult mathematicians experience when they contemplate shape and form and their properties is similar to the pleasure and joy that children experience when they build. Blocks give children an entry into a world where objects have predictable similarities and relations. They can be explored and experimented with and, because of their specific shape, be absolutely relied upon. With blocks, children can reproduce useful constructions from real life or create abstract designs to wonder and marvel at. Unknown to children, structures reflect concise mathematical relations. Children's pleasure in form and structure is mathematical in nature.

Since antiquity, there has been a mystery about geometric shapes and solids, felt by mathematicians and builders alike. The Greeks discovered that there are only five regular geometric solids. One of them is the cube. No matter which side of the cube faces you, its shape remains the same. It is uniquely symmetrical. The cube's cousin, the oblong block (in our case, the unit block), also exhibits mysteries of symmetry and regularity. It has a limited number of faces, edges, and corners. Its straitness and elongated form make it an ideal building material. It has played an important role in the architecture of Western and Eastern civilizations. The stone blocks used to build the pyramids were rectangular solids; the Incas used them in their long-lasting structures. The rectangle was put into particularly good use in the Greek temples, of which not only the foundation but the four sides were rectangular, the front a so-called golden rectangle. In modern life, most buildings make profuse use of the

When children build with blocks, they establish an experiential foundation of architecture and mathematics. Perhaps a future architect or mathematician will emerge!

build, an understanding that is the basis for the study of architecture and mathematics. There is a specific individuality and feeling about block construction as well. Suggest, for example, that two children use 10 blocks of the same kind. See what different kinds of structures they make. Perhaps a future architect will emerge! Frank Lloyd Wright said in his autobiography that in trying to trace the influences that led him to become an architect, the Froebelian kindergarten blocks he had used in the 1870s were the only things he could be enthusiastic and definite about.

The smooth, shapely maple blocks with which to build, the sense of which never afterwards left the fingers: so form became feeling. (1932, 11)

In their early years, children are in what Eileen Churchill (1961) calls the "age of comparisons." They find out about the world around them through an infinite number of comparisons. Their constructions permit them to compare height, length, width, shape, and number of blocks. To describe their world, children begin to use the language of mathematics.

Mathematics is a study of structures and systematic patterns of relationships. This kind of study is important for general abstract thinking. Children's ability to compare one thing with another is an important factor in their mental or cognitive development. We must, therefore, neither overestimate nor underestimate what hap-

rectangle in the shape of their bricks, the plan of the foundations and rooms, and the forms of doorways and windows.

Thus when children build with blocks, they establish an experiential foundation of architecture and mathematics. A relational understanding comes into play when children pens intellectually when children are building with blocks. They are accumulating experience with the almost infinite number of ways in which blocks can be related to one another. To support this process fully, we have to extend our knowledge both of mathematics and of general cognitive development. Only when we have a reasonably clear picture of what may (or may not) happen in children's perceptions and conceptions can we support their intellectual development. Perhaps we will find that the most important thing we can do is to observe and thereby appreciate the child's accomplishments.

Mathematics and geometry

Mathematics studies patterns and relationships. Our knowledge of mathematics as a structure and as a language is usually quite inadequate, although this weakness is not likely to be our fault. Many of us were exposed to a type of mathematics teaching and learning that did nothing to make us enthusiastic about the subject. Children develop mathematical concepts through comparisons, such as relating blocks to each other when building with them.

To most of us, *geometry* seems mainly to be associated with the naming of regular shapes, such as squares, triangles, and circles, perhaps including some of the regular solids—cubes, spheres, and so forth—imbued with properties and formulas from a long-forgotten school geometry. This belongs to a type of geometry mathematicians call *Euclidean geometry*. Euclid's geometry is a geometry of objects and, in the final analysis, is concerned with interrelationships between points, lines, and planes (to children, at their concrete stage of development, the relationships between corners, edges, and faces of blocks). It includes a geometry of size, shape, and measurement of height, length, area, volume, angles, etc.

Children, while playing with blocks, perceive and eventually conceptualize Euclidean notions inherent in the blocks and in the structures they build with them, but this happens only gradually. It is not the place where they start out in their geometrical and mathematical concept formation.

We have to explore some wider fields of geometry if we want to acquire a broader base of understanding of the geometric perceptions of children while building with blocks, namely the branches of mathematics called *topology* and *projective geometry*. Foreign as these terms may seem, they help us to understand the broad learning young children are involved in while they slowly develop Euclidean concepts. It is of particular interest to us here that it is these three geometric systems together—*Euclidean geometry, topology,* and *projective geometry*—that Piaget has used in his explorations of young children's developmental learning about space. Our field of study therefore carries us beyond unit blocks.

The beginning block builder deals first of all with the spatial relations of objects to each other, as described by the geometric system of *topology*. The topological concepts involved in block building include

• proximity (nearness), when objects are next to each other (i.e., "next to," "beside," "on"), and separation;

• seriation, ordering;

As children view their structure from various angles, they see how very different things look as perspective changes.

• surrounding, enclosure ("inside," "outside");

• continuum (i.e., surfaces are not in bits and pieces but are continuous); and

• dimensionality (i.e., space is three-dimensional; items are "on top of," "under," or "around" other objects).

Because objects—and their shapes—rarely are seen in full-plane view, *projective geometry* has been called the "geometry of viewpoints." It is concerned with seeing objects from differing sides and angles, or as seen in perspective, from near or far. The differing shapes that shadows make are part of the study of this type of geometry.

We can easily observe children's topological experiences. The ideas of inside and outside are part of the concepts of enclosure, or surrounding. Everyone is familiar with children's passion for the insides of things—for the opening and closing of boxes; for taking things out of a box, only to put them right back in again and secure the lid tightly, then repeat the whole procedure. Friedrich Froebel, the father of the kindergarten, was the first to document such observations from his work with young children in 1836 (Leeb-Lundberg 1972). And in New York in our day, a small boy walks into the kindergarten one morning, goes over to the block corner, takes out a few blocks, completely encircles a little floor space for himself, moves one block slightly to the side, walks in, closes the door, and sits quietly for 10 minutes. Then he opens the door and goes outside, relaxed and satisfied, to join the other children in play. Even more topological in nature is the wish of 5-year-old Tommy, who one day said to his teacher, "I wish I could dig a hole, crawl into it, and pull it into me!" When children do and say such things, they display an awareness of the inside/outside concept.

When a girl builds a little house with walls (perhaps under a table, so she has a good, stable roof for her enclosure) in order to creep into it and sit there with her best friend, she makes the real world conform to her bodily and emotional needs through the topological notion of inside. When she sits on top of a building and the house is under her, she is obviously outside it. The richness of her topological experience is strengthened by the fact that "on top of it" and "under" can be considered Euclidean concepts as well, through the child's beginning learning about *directions* in *space*. Whether the foundation of the house is a square, an irregular triangle, or a pentagon makes no difference to her—it is the enclosure that counts. Her "inside" and "outside" relate to anything she may build—a boat, an airplane, a car, a garage, and so on.

In all these instances, the different points of view from which children experience their structures (from inside, outside, in front of, in back of, etc.) make the shapes they contain constantly change as the children move about. The structure will seem different whether children are close to it or some distance away. The perspective, as well as the size, changes, and the blocks themselves look different as children turn the blocks around.

These experiences of perspective relate to projective geometry, which examines objects in relation to points of view. Children's struggles with projective ideas are evident in their drawings. They draw, for instance, a house from various points of view concurrently, or a face in profile but with two eyes.

While it is interesting for adults to observe and to understand the growth of topological, projective, and Euclidian viewpoints, the teacher is not expected to "help" these understandings to develop. In fact, it is not always easy for adults to be sure which geometric point of view is dominant in the child's work.

Development and insights

Children's ideas of space develop from their awareness of their own bodies and movements; in this respect children's conceptions of space are similar to notions held by early humans. Some terms used by primitive people suggest clearly that the body was the source of their spatial concepts (the word *eye* could indicate *before*, the word *back* could indicate *behind*, and the word *ground* also could mean *under*). Seen this way, a word like *floor* can be looked upon as a directional word for preschool children. They build on the floor all the time; it is always at the bottom of their structure and provides the basis for construction. Only much later, when children become able to conserve length (around age 8 or 9), does the notion that change of position can be related to a fixed reference point become central to the idea of measurement.

In preschool, children learn about space mainly by moving. Their movements include running, jumping, stretching, lifting, and putting down. The block corner may be *far away* at the other end of the room; they run to get *close* to it so they can take out the blocks and start building. They may stretch *high* to make their buildings *tall*. Their towers may be *close* to the wall or *next* to the window or dollhouse. They jump *down* from a ramp. The block corner may be *separated from* the entrance door by a bookcase or be *enclosed* by partitions.

Of course, children do not develop concepts in a strictly sequential fashion. Topological, projective, and Euclidean notions mix from quite early on, although the first basic adjustments infants make seem to be topological in nature—when they relate to the outside of their mothers, to their cribs, and to their own bodies with all their miraculous extremities that can stretch or clutch. The topological ideas of being near something or someone (mother) or of being less close (separation) become meaningful in terms of subjective experiences, sometimes with strong emotional force. Handling of objects leads to a certain knowledge of figures and shapes. Although very young children may be able to recognize and even name linear shapes such as squares and triangles, the image of these objects in their minds has been proven to be vague. In fact, Piaget has shown that children identify shapes that display topological relationships, such as rounded forms, more readily than they identify Euclidean straight-sided shapes. This finding is intriguing in light of the fact that rounded forms, such as the mother's face and body, are closer to nature.

Piagetian perspectives

Based on extensive studies of children's logical and mathematical thinking, Piaget (e.g., 1967) concludes that children cannot be "taught" mathematical understandings through verbal instruction. Repeating numbers by rote does not help them to develop concepts of quantity. What children need is hands-on interaction with many kinds of materials. Blocks require no prescribed action and allow children to *invent* their knowledge through manipulation.

Children of approximately 2 to 7 years old are in what Piaget calls the time of *preoperational thought,* when reasoning can take place only through action (Piaget & Inhelder 1967). When building with blocks, children at this stage develop a beginning mathematical understanding in a number of areas, as suggested by Saunders and Bingham-Newman (1984):

• comparisons—e.g., recognizing differences in height, width, shape, weight, and between "more," "less," "the same";

• seriation—e.g., ordering by size, constructing steps;

• correspondence—such as making construction size fit dolls, trucks, etc.;

• classification—e.g., matching, sorting;

• part–whole relationships—such as recognizing subunits and smaller patterns within the construction, relation of individual blocks to the structure; seeing component parts again when buildings are dismantled or when they collapse;

- grouping—such as adding identical-size blocks to buildings, cleaning up by twos or threes;
- estimation—judging quantity of materials needed for buildings, space needed; and
- measurement—e.g., being aware of space needed, height, length, volume.

Piaget describes young preoperational children as *egocentric*—that is, they are not able to take the point of view of another person. Beginning block builders work alone or engage in parallel play. But over time they begin to *decenter*, taking the ideas of others into consideration.

The reasoning of preoperational children is influenced by their perceptual activities. Their thought is tied to perception. Their actions become internalized through representational activities such as block building. As children grapple with the problems they encounter in building, they begin to apply previous learnings. They will be able to apply logical thought processes (operations)—based on past experiences—to problems as they come up. When they become able to reason without depending on actions, they enter the next stage of development, *concrete operations* (at about age 7 to 11) (Piaget & Inhelder 1967).

Generally, children's ability to talk about what they are doing follows their ability to do it. Gradually language and action begin to merge. An increasing awareness of the significance of her experience brings the child to naming or accepting a word given by an adult at the right moment—that is, when the adult notes that the concept is already in the child's mind. Such words as *up, down, over, under, above, below, before,* and *behind* seem to be necessary language tools. It is difficult for children to discuss spatial relationships without using these words. Most preschool children also understand the words *on top* and *behind;* at age 5, many children also understand the terms *backward* and *forward.* But only 60% of 5-year-olds showed that they understood the difference between *tiny* and *huge,* and fewer than one half could show that they understood the difference between *far* and *near* (Lovell 1964).

Actions as they are performed on the objects bring about a more conceptual development. It is for this reason that building activities with blocks (and other concrete materials) are so important. When children acquire a repertoire of actions, they accumulate experiences of the effects of these actions. In Piaget's formulation, thought arises from the *interior-ization* of actions. Geometrical thought itself is a system of internalized actions. When children attain the ability to mentally represent spatial relationships that are not directly observable, their actions build systems of mental operations with which they are better able to interpret the world. It is interesting to note that children's beginning efforts in block building are efforts to make representations of real things in the physical world. Froebel observed this phenomenon and called these structures that children make— of houses, furniture, and other common objects—"forms of life" (Leeb-Lundberg 1972).

When children attain the concrete operations stage, they are able to think about mental processes in a new way (Piaget & Inhelder 1967). They become able, specifically, to do what Piaget calls *conserve* (which will be discussed later) and are able to reverse their thinking—that is, to go back to the starting point and think through the process.

How preoperational children may struggle with the idea of reversibility—when they have not yet reached the developmental stage in which they can internalize the actions preceding this concept—is illustrated by a child who, while visiting the zoo, was taken up one flight of stairs and down another. The next day, when visiting the zoo again, she was taken up by the stairs she had previously come down. She protested that these were "going down" stairs and the others were "going up" stairs. Another story tells about a 7-year-old who had been taken for a long, circular walk through the woods. When the boy and his companion were almost home again, they saw a strawberry patch. The following day the boy tried to walk with his mother from the house directly to the patch, but he was unable to do so. Instead he had to make the circular journey through the woods, as on the day before, until once again he came across the strawberries. Relying on a sequential chain of associations and memories, the child was not yet able to reverse his thinking (Lovell 1964).

True *reversibility* means, in Piaget's (1963) view, that children are able to reverse their thinking about actions they have performed—that is, to go back to the point where they began and think through their experience. The children in the preceding stories could not think this way yet; they were still in the preoperational stage.

These rather surprising stories about young children's thinking ought to put us into the observer's place rather than the teacher's. It is important to realize the psychological development that children are going through

so that in our eagerness to accelerate learning we do not try to "teach" children things that they can construct only in their own minds, with the aid of a multitude of first-hand experiences. Research has made it abundantly clear that concept formation cannot be forced. All children have to pass through certain developmental stages in their conceptual development, stages that are related to their chronological and mental age and past experience. For some children the process takes a long time; for others it happens more quickly.

With care, however, teachers can use blocks to find out whether a child is able to analyze a construction she has made so that she can reverse the process she used in building it. A child can be encouraged to look carefully and see how her structure was put together, then take it apart and reconstruct it. The degree of difficulty, of course, will depend upon how elaborate the original construction was. It also might be interesting to observe how children spontaneously sort blocks—for example, by shape or size.

To realize fully the amount of intuitive learning that is involved when children play with blocks, we also must be aware of what Piaget calls *conservation*. Up to 6, 7, or even 8 years of age, most children appear to not understand that the amount or quantity (e.g., of blocks, raisins, buttons, or clay) stays the same, regardless of changes in shape, position, or rearrangement. If we consider the set of unit blocks, another surprising conclusion can therefore be drawn from Piaget's experiments with children. Four- to 6-year-olds (sometimes even older children) are apt to believe that once they have taken all the blocks off the shelves and built a large, spread-

Children's perception of stability can be seen when they test their structure by placing a block gingerly or by placing it tentatively.

out construction on the floor, they have more blocks than when the same blocks were stored in a compact way on the shelves. In other words, they center their attention on only one aspect of the situation at a time—in this case, on the floor space the blocks occupy rather than on the actual amount of pieces involved. They cannot conserve the amount.

When children build they constantly accumulate experiences with the different ways in which objects can be related to one another. This becomes the foundation for a multitude of mathematical concepts, not only that of number. Conservation, for example, relates also to the geometric concepts of length, area, and volume. The fact that these concepts are generally not fully attained until after kindergarten age does not belittle the children's preschool and kindergarten experience; in fact, the richer the underlying reservoir of past experiences, the more easily children will be able to conceptualize abstractions, once they are mature enough to do so. With age and experience children gradually come to appreciate the mathematical meanings of their actions through their constant rearranging of the materials they use in their constructions, whether they have made houses, ships, towers, or highways.

Mathematical and geometric concepts

Mathematical concepts develop through activity. In block building we often find that children's activities deal with the problem of whether the number of blocks, the length of the road, or other measure of quantity remains the same, no matter what the position of the objects. This again relates, in young children, to movement. Either the object is moved around or the child's body moves in relation to the object.

Length and height. When children begin to work with blocks, they usually put them together flat on the floor, a few pieces at a time, first one block, then another, and then another. Later, blocks laid end to end become a road or a railroad track. When children discover that they can pile the blocks on top of each other, building *up, high,* this is quite a surprise for them. The repetitive activity of arranging blocks in towers and rows can absorb children for a long time. To lay one block upon another may be, for some children, a simpler process than to place them next to one another in a line (although some 2-year-old children have been observed to build towers and rows the first month they were given blocks to play with). Eventually these experiences lead to the concept of length, which includes the horizontal width and the vertical height and depth.

Children younger than age 5 usually experience comparisons, such as *this is longer than that* or *that is higher than this,* rather than actual lengths. These expressions about inequality of length are associated with many experiences. They can range from the length of fingers to the height of mountains. Children usually use their own body as a reference in relation to other objects. They experience that what is high or tall as relative— their block towers may be high, but so is the Empire State Building. To say that something is *longer* or *shorter* is easier for the child than to say it is *the same length* or *as long as*

Six-year-old Tommy was asked about the submarine he had made. He said it was for one boy inside and one on top. When asked how he could make the inside large enough for two boys, he immediately suggested making the model longer by adding one more block at each end.

For Tommy, obviously, *bigger* meant *longer*. He was not yet able to consider more than one dimension at a time.

The individual blocks, of course, exhibit simple length relationships as well.

During block building I asked 4-year-old Kelli to find a block that was longer than the one I placed on the floor. The block on the floor was a half unit. She selected a double unit.

One of Piaget's experiments showed that 4-year-old children do not use the word *straight* and have difficulty constructing a straight line. When asked to make one, they instead construct a wavy or curved line. This also can be observed when children work with unit blocks. At about the age of 6, however, the child can sight along the line from one end and therefore is able to make the line straight. The relative ease with which the wide unit blocks can be fitted together gives children working with them many experiences with straight lines.

Children are faced with the problem of equivalence of length—that lines may be equally long even when they differ in shape or angle. When children build railroad tracks and use curved as well as oblong unit blocks, the following lengths will be about equivalent:

As they build with blocks, children encounter many situations in which they need to compare or measure.

(equality of length). From their play and by watching grownups, children also may experience that a stick can be shortened by breaking it or that blocks can be joined to other blocks to make longer tracks or trains or, as in the following case, submarines.

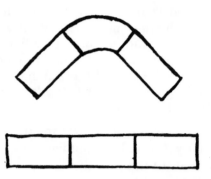

Specific experiments designed by Piaget (1967) have shown that children have difficulty realizing that the length of two identical lines (or blocks, representing lengths) put in different position remains the same.

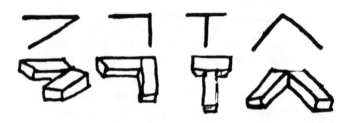

Length also can mean perimeter, for example, an outline of a foundation for a building. In the following cases both perimeters, as measured by unit blocks, are the same, although they may appear to be different:

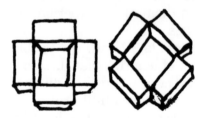

Not until about the age of 7 are children able to conserve length—that is, realize that the length is the same no matter what the arrangement of the individual blocks used.

To understand the measurement of length, one must be able to conserve length. The child also needs to understand that a whole consists of a number of parts added together and that length can be measured in terms of other lengths—that is, through the repeated application of a unit of measure. The essence of measurement is, again, *comparison* of the item to be measured with the unit of measure. This unit of measure is arbitrary. The unit blocks can be measured in terms of other unit blocks, but they also can be measured in terms of handspans, thumbprints, or straws put end to end. Conceptually, measurement is the synthesis of division into parts and of what Piaget calls *iteration* (repetition) of the unit (Piaget & Inhelder 1967).

Young children have no understanding of lengths in terms of other lengths. One of Piaget's experiments involved studying children's spontaneous measurement at different ages (Piaget, Inhelder, & Szeminska 1964). The text of this experiment will be quoted at length because it is one of the few experiments in which Piaget used blocks and because it gives good insight into the developmental levels of children.

> The experimenter showed the child a tower made of twelve blocks and a little over 2 feet 6 inches high—the tower being constructed on a table. The experimenter told the child to make another tower "the same as mine" on another table about 6 feet away, the table top being some 3 feet lower than that of the first

table. There was a large screen between the model and the copy but the child was encouraged to "go and see" the model as often as he liked. He was also given strips of paper, sticks, rulers, etc., and he was told to use them if his spontaneous efforts ceased, but he was NOT told how to use them. The following stages were observed:

(a) up to about 4½ years of age there was visual comparison only. The child judged the second tower to be the same height as the first by stepping back and estimating height. This was done regardless of the difference in heights of the table tops.

(b) from 4½ to 7 years the child might lay a long rod across the tops of the towers to make sure they were level. When he realized that the bases of the towers were not at the same height, he sometimes attempted to place his tower on the same table as the model. Naturally, that was not permitted. Later, the children began to look for a measuring instrument, and some of them began using their own bodies for this purpose. For example, the span of the hands might be used, or the arms, by placing one hand on top of the model tower and the other at the base and moving over from the model to the copy, meanwhile trying to keep the hands the same distance apart. When they discovered that this procedure was unreliable, some would place, say, their shoulder against the top of the tower (a chair or stool might be used) and would make a spot on their leg opposite the base. They would then move to the second tower to see if the heights were the same.

(c) from 7 years onwards there was an increasing tendency to use some symbolic object (e.g., a rod) to imitate size. Very occasionally a child built a third tower by the first and carried it over to the second: this was permitted. More frequently, though, he used a rod that was exactly the *same length* as the model tower was high. (Piaget, Inhelder, & Szeminska 1964)

The preoperational child was able to match identical lengths—an intelligent beginning of comparison. Children sometimes used a stick that was shorter than the tower, however. This stick was applied to the tower the necessary number of times. The height of the model tower was then obtained by repeatedly using the shorter stick as a means of measurement. This, of course, meant that the concept of measurement of length was finally formed.

It is of particular interest that some of the children began to use their own bodies as instruments for measuring or in some way related a body part to the height of the tower. Our traditional standard system of measure in the United States, the yard system, originated with people using different parts of their bodies as measures; children's instinctive notions about measurement are similar to the conceptions of early civilizations.

To build a tower as tall as oneself is a good means of finding equal lengths. Games using handspans, paces, feet, or body lengths (children stretched out in a line on the floor) to measure the length of a construction or the room are enjoyable activities for children. Unit blocks also can be used as units of measure to find out how long or how tall a building is (although there is no need to use the term *measure* with children when they are experimenting with this strategy!). More advanced children could *make* a measuring stick, calibrated according to blocks and painted. Mathematicians recommend that children begin to learn about measurements using this kind of arbitrary unit, so well suited to their subjective experiences. To make the activities richer, children who are ready can first estimate or guess how many blocks or handspans will be needed. The following example shows how 5- and 6-year-olds use their bodies for comparison in finding out about height and how they use blocks as arbitrary units of measure. Dick and Johnny are 5; Bill and Jonathan, 6.

> Dick and Johnny built towers. Johnny said his was the highest. He measured his by standing up. Dick also stood up. He said he was as high as Johnny and Johnny's tower higher than his. Dick then tried to build his up higher, but Bill and Jonathan built towers, too, and Bill said they were both the same. They discussed this, and quadruple units were used to prove who was right.

Beginning measurement also can be taught by comparing a child's construction with other objects in the room. A piece of string or rope beside the structure can become a unit of measurement. Comparative terms can be used as the length of string is matched to various objects: "Your building is longer than the table" or "It is higher than the shelf." Or a question can be asked, such as, "Can you find something that is as long as your block?" Next, the teacher can help to measure it to see how nearly correct the child was.

When using the blocks, matching smaller pieces to larger ones (constantly occurring when building walls, for example) involves a certain spontaneous measurement of length (or matching of size). Thus, if the quadruple unit is compared with the unit block, it is found to be equal to four unit blocks; likewise, two unit blocks equal one double unit.

> Erick, who was building an airport, could find only double units on the storage shelves. The double units were not long enough to reach across the walls of the airport to make a roof. He took two of the double units to Ricky and said, "I'll let you have these two blocks if you give me one of your long blocks. Look, you can use these two blocks in your wall—they'll just fit where you have this long one." They traded the blocks. Later Ricky offered all his quadruple units for every two double units that Erick gave him.

This kind of experience leads, of course, in the direction of the concept of fractions—halves, fourths, and so on. This subject is further discussed in the section "Some mathematical features of the Pratt blocks," starting on page 55.

Area. The word *area* may be defined, on a child's level, as the amount of surface or, in the case of the outline of a house, a car, or a boat that the child builds, simply as the amount of floor space. Children frequently enclose areas in their play; enclosed outline forms are among the simple beginning structures they make. Every building made of blocks has a foundation that defines its area; the shape is easily perceived by the child. It does not have to be square or rectangular; an odd-shaped building, such as a pentagonal or L-shaped one, may be even more interesting. In all cases the size of the foundation determines the area of the floor space the building occupies.

Before they begin building with blocks, children encounter many situations in which an amount of surface comes within their view. Their mattress is covered with sheets and a blanket. They see floors, doors, windows, tabletops, tiles, and blocks—all of which display a surface. At the easel, they cover a sheet of paper with poster paint. Slowly they build in their minds some notion of area or size of surface. They notice that some surfaces are larger than others or that there is more room on some surfaces than on others. They love to work on the surface they call the floor. They feel its bigness. They discover that areas not only have different sizes but also are different in shape. By comparing two tables of different shape but of about the same area, children again may center on one aspect of the problem at a time, such as the length, and say that the longer surface is also the bigger one. Even when they have acquired the concept of area, they, like some adults, may not formulate insight clearly and may say that one table is bigger than the other when they mean that its area is bigger.

Young children gain many useful experiences with unit blocks that give them a foundation for operational understanding of area later. In their continual experimentation with blocks, children find out which surfaces fit well together, which blocks make the best walls or roofs, and which surfaces balance best. They find out that the blocks with the largest surface make the best foundations for their structures and that some of the blocks with smaller surfaces, if joined together, can fit on top of the larger surfaces. It will take a long time, however, before they can calculate the area of, say, a rectangle. Their ideas will eventually have to apply either to an area that is surrounded by an outline (a corral, a doorway, a window frame) or to an area filled in or covered with blocks. They will have to be able, as with length, to *conserve* area, no matter what the shape of the structure or the arrangement of the individual blocks. In other words, they have to be able to assimilate the fact that the following sets of blocks could be arranged to cover the same amount of surface.

The regular properties of the blocks provide opportunities for recurring experiences that lead toward conservation of area. A unit block "standing up" may at first appear different to children from the same block "lying down." They are apt to believe that the block standing up is larger than the one lying down, their attention now centering on the height.

The small right-angle triangle (one half of one-half the unit block) has one longer and two shorter sides. The shape is not necessarily perceived as the same when children see the triangle resting on its longer side.

When children are building they may discover that two triangles can combine to form a rectangle or square.

On another occasion the same pieces may be joined together in a different way to form, say, a rooftop.

An interesting transformation has now taken place: the two smaller triangles have made one larger triangle (the area, of course, is still the same).

A Piagetian experiment to investigate the child's specific understanding called for using two similar triangular shapes cut from a cardboard square. The child was asked to make a large triangle out of the two smaller ones. It was found that 5- and 6-year-olds tended to believe that the new triangle was bigger than the original square. Six- to 7-year-olds made better judgments, although they could formulate them only intuitively. From about age 7, however, children conserved area and gave good reasons why they believed that the area had not changed.

While going through experiences that lead toward the concept of area, children have unconcerned fun with areas of all kinds. As they build houses, garages, airports, barns, and stables, they are deeply involved in mathematics without being aware that they are. As they cover a floor space or build a wall, they often work with patterns. A simple pattern may be made by putting unit blocks together. The patterns are often symmetrical and show that the children perceive the area relationships that appear among the blocks.

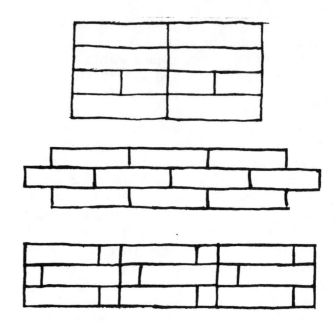

In the following unusual and balanced arrangement, the double units are framed by quadruple units and the total area is well defined.

The beauty and the wonder of fitting shapes so exactly is the child's main interest in this activity.

In mathematics, the repeated application of shapes to cover a surface is called a *tessellation*, as in the wall patterns just shown. In the act of covering a surface, the child is intuitively using the half and double units as units of measure for the total surface.

On occasion the teacher may want to give children a specific challenge. For instance, she may limit the number of blocks used to 10 or 12 half units or units and ask, "How many differently shaped bathroom floors can you lay out with these blocks?" Or children may be invited to experiment with the blocks by constructing rectangular or square forms of various sizes. They may discover that whether these figures are put horizontally or vertically, they still make rectangular shapes, or the teacher may draw children's attention to this fact.

Volume. It is easy to notice how children, when handling the blocks, gain increasing familiarity with three-dimensional volume relationships.

Although children do not arrive at these concepts operationally until after the age of 10, activities with blocks prepare (and promote) children's conceptions—in fact, because acquiring this concept is difficult, children's need for physical experiences is greater. Children also encounter this type of experience when they play with sand, water, and other materials that can be poured into containers.

Putting away blocks affords opportunities to make good use of certain available spaces. With practice and experience, the children learn how the individual pieces fill the shelf completely. When building with blocks, children make airports in which each plane has

As children cover a floor space or build a wall, they often work with patterns.

to fit into its own hangar, or garages that have to hold several cars. Caroline Pratt and Jessie Stanton describe an incident in which children are struggling to make a stable big enough for a horse.

A toy horse, returned to school by someone and left on the window seat, was instantly seen by Diana. I said she could have it when she made a stable for it. She and Elizabeth, a new child this year, both began to build. Elizabeth made a tiny construction, but could not put the horse into it. It did not occur to her to change the size of the stable. Diana, on the other hand, having built a large stable with a low roof, after several attempts to force the horse in, removed the blocks composing the roof, made the walls higher, and replaced the roof. She then tried to put into words what she had done, saying, "Roof too small." I gave her the words "high" and "low," and she went about the room smiling and repeating the explanation to the other children. (Pratt & Stanton 1926, 30–31)

This example illustrates how children are working in more than one dimension when volume relationships are involved and how they constructively approach one variable at a time (first height, then width). The activity also may occur when children find the volume of the inner space of, for example, a well they have built by discovering the number of unit blocks that can fill the well. Building houses and other objects also helps the children perceive that a structure takes up a certain amount of space.

Teachers must remember that volume is puzzling to a child, as illustrated by the following example:

Three 5-year-old children made towers. They counted the number of blocks in each and found that the highest tower did not have the most blocks.

In another instance a teacher observed two 5-year-olds who were trying to decide which was the bigger of two model cars. The dimensions of each were so similar that at long last they put the cars on a scale to find out, by weight, which one was larger.

One teacher reports that she occasionally gave to 5-year-olds problems such as the following: "Make a wall that is four blocks long, two blocks high, and one block thick" or "Make a wall that is two blocks deep" or "Make a box that is two blocks square." At the preoperational stage, children best approach problems one at a time. This teacher's first suggestion is too hard for most 5-year-olds, although it could provide a challenge for some. A simpler task may be to ask children to make equivalences of various blocks to equal a quadruple unit with smaller blocks ("Can you use these small blocks to make a wall as long as this?").

Number. We have seen, then, that young children's ideas of size and shape and their possible internal equivalences are mixed up, or in a state of disequilibrium, in regard to length, area, and volume. They move slowly, also, toward a state of equilibrium in regard to the concept of number. The development of the concept of number should be promoted through a multitude of experiences, using a great variety of materials: buttons, shells, pinecones, acorns, pegs, spoons, straws, dishes, and so forth.

Of course, number experiences are inherent in the use of blocks. A prerequisite for the development of the idea of number is a beginning appreciation that some sets of things are smaller than others, some are larger, and some are the same size. Experiences with equivalence and inequivalence occur frequently with blocks, mainly in relation to length, area, and volume. The same experiences also strengthen the ideas of "more" and "less," especially when comparing sets, groups, or piles of discrete objects or blocks.

Before Susan (5½ years old) started to build, she sorted the different shapes and sizes and put them into separate piles.

As the child takes all the small triangles and stacks them, she eventually comes to think of all these blocks together and, after some time, forms the concept of a set or class of all the smallest blocks. The child also may come to perceive that the total set of unit blocks contains more blocks than the set of triangular blocks, or pillars, or other individual shapes.

Other simple experiences of quantity with the blocks come about when children ask for more blocks to build with—many more! They might add that they need more because they do not have enough blocks to make their tower high. When asked how many blocks they used in a large structure, children may not necessarily count the blocks but simply say they used *a lot*—a good beginning and ancient quantitative word. Other ancient and similarly quantitative words are *heap, pile, stack,* and *mound*. Many of children's early block-building experiences, then, are of a basic quantitative nature.

Soon children make efforts to count—after all, many adults around them seem to think that counting is the main (or only) approach to learning number! The process of learning numbers *does* include counting, but it is more complex and interesting than that. A child may be able to count but still have no real concept of numbers. The ideas of *more, less,* and *the same as* are more basic.

Piaget has demonstrated that a child may be able to count objects and still not realize that the number of objects is unchanged when the objects are arranged in a new configuration. The following is a typical Piagetian experiment with the unit blocks:

The child makes a row of five blocks on the floor. He lays out another row next to it with the same number of blocks. He is then asked to check the number of blocks by matching them, using one-to-one correspondence, so that he is absolutely sure that the two rows contain the same number of blocks. Then the teacher spreads out the blocks in one of the rows so that the simple visual correspondence is lost.

Children younger than 6 or even 7, when asked, usually no longer agree that the two rows are still of equal length. Their perception leads them to believe that the amount in the spread-out row is now larger—that is, they center their attention on one dimension of the problem, namely, the new and larger space the blocks occupy. They cannot yet grasp that a number stands for a class or a set of things irrespective of the arrangement of the things within the set.

Another important property of numbers is that they can be compared with one another and put in order of magnitude. By the age of 3 or 4, children have an intuitive grasp of ordering (shown through their play with nesting toys and by putting graduated rings on sticks). They need to know that three is greater than two but less than four, and that six comes between five and seven. Children, therefore, need a great deal of experience in ordering, that is, in arranging a series of things according to their numerical or size differences. Piaget (1967) has shown that up to about 5 years of age, children are unable to make a series or a set of five or six or seven blocks of increasing length. At about age 6 they begin to put things in order using a process of trial and error, but if a block is omitted, it becomes difficult for the children to put it into the right place in the series or in the order they are trying to establish. However, by age 7, most children can identify the shortest block, then the next shortest, and so on.

To some children, ordering is very difficult. They need practice in putting blocks and other objects in order of size, for example, from the half unit to the quadruple unit. They also need to do this in reverse, starting with the big instead of the little block.

Children have not achieved the full idea of number until they have synthesized, in their own minds, the two ideas of grouping into sets (classification) and ordering of sets (seriation). *Classification* implies bunching similar things together. Thus, piling two, three, or five blocks of identical size on top of each other when putting them away will help children develop the concepts of "two," "three," or "five." *Seri-ation,* on the other hand, deals with a sequence of objects or numbers. For example, if the blocks are used as stairs, children may be able to say that the doll has reached the "first," "second," "fifth," or "last" step on the staircase. Although the cardinal and ordinal meanings of numbers are closely related for the child, in this period of disequilibrium the two concepts do not always coincide. Children may therefore be at the concrete-operational stage of thinking in one aspect but not yet in another.

Because blocks give opportunities for sorting, classifying, counting, and ordering, they become valuable material in the process of establishing the concept of number.

Because of this developmental process, then, children need a great deal of experience of a diverse nature to establish the number concept. Because blocks provide opportunities for sorting, classifying, counting, and ordering, they become valuable material in this process. Experience with equivalent sets, for example, takes place when children (or teachers) devise games for transporting blocks to the shelves ("Let's carry piles of five today").

In the following examples, we must remember that the ability to count does not ensure that the child has a concept of quantity.

> Jonathan counted how many blocks he had used. The rest of the children got interested and also counted theirs.

> Mary put seven blocks down. She said it was a street. She next put four blocks to be the houses along her street. She counted the houses: "One, two, three, four." She counted the rest of the blocks in the street and said, "I need three more houses." Mary is beginning to deal with the equivalence of quantity by practicing one-to-one correspondence.

Some mathematical features of Pratt blocks

Caroline Pratt called her blocks "free materials." In doing so, she was justifiably reacting to the rigid didactic use of Montessori and Froebelian materials of her day.

> In calling these materials *free* materials I can best distinguish them from the materials of the kindergarten and the Montessori schools. Their uses are various. They are not designed for some specific educational purpose of an adult, but are incidental to child life and child purpose. (Pratt 1917, 13)

After the misconceptions that had made the early American kindergarten stagnant, Caroline Pratt revitalized the Froebelian concept of learning through self-activity so that it is, to this day, very much alive. The fact that a whole section of this book is devoted to the mathematical development children go through while building with blocks reflects our desire to understand children's cognitive learning in all its aspects.

Variety of size and accompanying flexibility in use are, of course, the basic factors in the child's satisfaction with block building. The original shapes and sizes were undoubtedly selected because of their volumetric relationships and consequent usefulness for making intricate constructions. Most larger blocks in the set can be replaced in volume with combinations of other blocks. The set consists of a comparatively large number of unit blocks and fewer quadruple units. This forces block builders to substitute several unit blocks, for example, for one quadruple unit when the supply of large blocks is exhausted. Most of the solids in the set are equivalent in width and thickness, making them useful in displaying equivalence relations, an important class of relations in mathematics.

The basic piece in the set is called the *unit block*. This is the most commonly occurring block in the set, the one to which most of the others are related. In the set of Pratt blocks, there also are quarter units, half units, double units, and quadruple units (for pictures, see Appendix 2). These pieces, when matched, display fractional relationships easily seen when put together lengthwise, as in the following pattern, in which sets of smaller blocks are matched against the quadruple unit (sometimes called the *quadlong*). Halves, fourths, eights, and sixteenths appear as follows in relation to the quadlong:

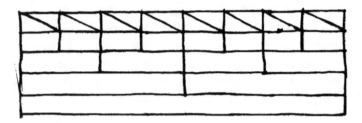

The square block is traditionally called the *half unit*. However, mathematically, the pillars are also halves of the unit block.

Another way of creating a unit block is with two of the large triangles, which then become halves of the unit block.

Or a unit block can be made with two of the small ramps.

Mathematically, there is a richness in seeing halves of the same thing in so many different ways. It also provides a good experience toward acquiring the conception of conserva-

tion of quantity, because each of these halves is inherently equivalent to every other.

Blocks that represent fractions in the set, however, have to be seen in relation to the unit block in any configuration. The following shapes show another way of seeing halves (also thirds and fourths) of rectangular areas:

Equivalence of volume is, of course, inherent in these and other configurations. If two half units are put on top of each other, they are still equivalent to the unit block, although the shape (or amount of wood) now looks different.

The same applies to many other structures that can be made with the blocks. Four small triangles put on top of each other contain the same amount of wood as one unit block. Two small triangles on top of each other are equivalent to one half unit; 8 small triangles are equivalent to one double unit; 16 small triangles are equivalent to one quadruple unit (See top of page 57).

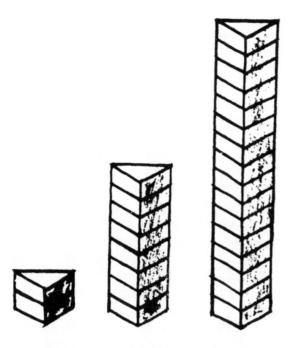

To prove these last equivalent relations, it is necessary only to match the triangular pieces lengthwise with the oblong blocks with which they are compared.

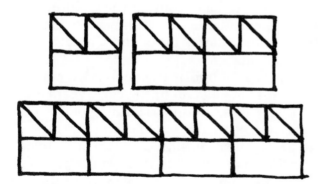

This approach to a mathematical proof is legitimate to a mathematician—a proof being what makes *sense* at a particular level of intellectual development.

Using blocks presents children with many opportunities to make discoveries about shapes. A multitude of configurations appear from children's spontaneous arrangements. Four of the small triangles can make a square:

Four of the large triangles can make a rhombus:

Two squares and four small triangles make a hexagon:

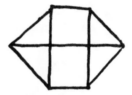

Two triangles joined to a square or rectangle make a parallelogram:

Or two small triangles and a square create a trapezoid (the long side of the trapezoid may be at the top or bottom; if the long side is at the top, the children may call it a boat):

57

Shapes and forms in one, two, or three dimensions can be illustrated indefinitely through the mathematical model that the set of blocks constitutes. The following example also is written as an arithmetical statement to show the implications (in children's constructions) for later formal work with whole numbers and fractions:

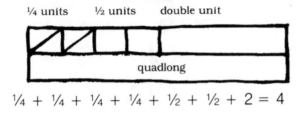

$$\frac{1}{4} + \frac{1}{4} + \frac{1}{4} + \frac{1}{4} + \frac{1}{2} + \frac{1}{2} + 2 = 4$$

These arithmetical facts are apparent whether the blocks are put end to end, as in the picture, or used freely in building, such as in the following ship, which is made from the same blocks as the figure above. The ship, then, is equivalent to the quadruple unit in length, area, volume, and the length of its constituent units.

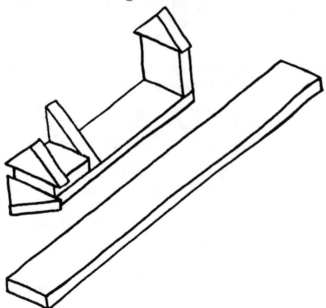

This kind of direct experience relating to conservation is one of the most important mathematical experiences that children have in building with unit blocks.

The teacher

It has been stressed throughout this chapter how interesting and rewarding it can be to study children's perceptions (and conceptions) as experienced in their block play. Children develop ideas about mathematics from form—this is what opens their minds.

Round blocks (such as cylinders), for example, roll. When children see them rolling, something happens in their minds. Their conception of space and geometric form moving through space changes. In contrast, square or rectangular blocks can only be pushed; there is no momentum in the square. The kind of blocks we give to children determines, in a certain sense, the type of creative imagination that comes into play when children build. At some point in the children's development, the teacher will need to gradually introduce more blocks and a greater variety of shapes.

In the type of informal, open-ended education that should go on in the early years of children's lives, an understanding of the underlying structure of children's learning and development is vital. The teacher's role regarding block building is not a difficult one if he or she knows what is inherent in the material. The teacher will then know how to extend the experiences of the children and ask the right questions or pose a new problem. Of course, in this process the adult needs to know where the individual child is developmentally—this is what developmental learning is all about. Encouragement of children's trial-and-error learning and appreciation of their struggle help teachers to understand and have the right attitude toward children who develop at a different rate.

By asking and responding to questions, the teacher can help children discover the differences and similarities among things. Such relational thinking is the essence of mathematics as a structure. The teacher may take pictures of a construction from different angles to emphasize projective geometric aspects and let children look and make comments. However, children are constantly involved in nonverbal questions of their own, and they generally cannot see or talk with the same specificity as can an adult. The things that children actually understand are those things that are of real value to them and those that they can use in future constructions.

Children's purposes are sometimes better served if the teacher resists being specific about what a building looks like to him or her. If a child names a structure, accept the name, no matter how incongruous it may seem. The true purpose of children's buildings is not always representational but experimental. Children seek to find out what the material will do and what they can do with it. On the other hand, a teacher may be deceived because a child may use the appropriate word and still have no idea about the concept it relates to.

However, language does play a very important role, because most concepts are developed with some kind of verbalization. To

Our aim for mathematician block builders should be to make it possible for them to use their mathematical and architectural creativity so that their interest and spontaneous pleasure in what they are doing are kept alive.

understand how things are related, children must be given words that describe likenesses and differences. This specialized, broad, mathematical vocabulary provides them with further means for experimenting, thinking, and reasoning about relationships: each new word may focus on a relationship. At the same time, we should not force children to verbalize about their constructions. Meaningful language development comes naturally and often represents a summation of some new insight based on innumerable experiences. The language of the adult is truly accepted by children only if it lies within the circle of their experiences and ideas. This is, again, where our listening and observing become so important. What children do with blocks shows extraordinary variety, as do their verbal exchanges about their constructions. The mathematical language from the adult has to be provided at the right time so that it helps a concept to develop appropriately; if this language is used too soon, it may hinder the development of the concept.

We have to remember that children develop these concepts as if going into a cave. They don't know what is in it. The cave is empty—only after they go in do they start to discover. There may be a square, a triangle, and a cylinder inside. The children experience each of these shapes individually. They are surprised at what is in the cave. They start absorbing in their minds the dimensions of the objects. From the impressions they receive, they intuitively start building. Children's perceptions, intuition, and activity lead them toward the concepts. Their driving force is curiosity.

Our aim for mathematician block builders should be to make it possible for them to use their mathematical and architectural creativity so that their interest and spontaneous pleasure in what they are doing are kept alive.

References

Churchill, E.M. 1961. *Counting and measuring: An approach to number education in the infant school.* Toronto: Toronto University Press.

Johnson, H.M. [1933] 1966. *The art of block building.* New York: Bank Street College of Education.

Leeb-Lundberg, K. 1970. Kindergarten mathematics laboratory—nineteenth century fashion. *The Arithmetic Teacher 17* (5): 372–86.

Leeb-Lundberg, K. 1972. Friedrich Froebel's mathematics for the kindergarten. Philosophy, program and implementation in the United States. Ph.D. diss., New York University.

Lovell, K. 1964. *The growth of basic mathematical and scientific concepts in children.* London: University of London Press.

Lovell, K. 1971. *The growth of understanding in mathematics: Kindergarten through grade three.* New York: Holt, Rinehart, & Winston.

Piaget, J. 1963. *The psychology of intelligence.* Patterson, NJ: Littlefield Adams.

Piaget, J. 1967. *The child's conception of number.* New York: W.W. Norton.

Piaget, J., & B. Inhelder. 1967. *The child's conception of space.* London: Routledge & Kegan Paul.

Piaget, J., B. Inhelder, & A. Szeminska. 1964. *The child's conception of geometry.* New York: Harper-Collins.

Pratt, C. 1917. *The play school: An experiment in education.* (Bureau of Educational Experiments Bulletin No. 3). New York: Bank Street College of Education.

Pratt, C., & J. Stanton. 1926. *Before books.* New York: Adelphi.

Saunders, R., & A. Bingham-Newman. 1984. *Piagetian perspective for preschools: A thinking book for teachers.* Englewood Cliffs, NJ: Prentice Hall.

Wright, F.L. 1932. *An autobiography.* New York: Longman.

5

Social Studies through Block Building

Charlotte Brody and Elisabeth S. Hirsch

Egocentricity

Contemplating primary-age children tackling the complex problems of social living becomes awe inspiring when we consider that barely six or seven years ago, those children hardly grasped their own identity and were unable to understand the existence of others.

Mahler (1968) describes the inability of infants to understand that their mother is not part of themselves. According to Piaget (1926), young children are unable to grasp that other people have thoughts, viewpoints, or feelings different from their own. This egocentricity is often mislabeled as selfishness, rudeness, or inconsiderateness. It is none of these. Only with the ability to understand how other people feel can it become possible to selfishly disregard those feelings.

Egocentric thought affects children's conception of space as well. Infants are unable to grasp that objects remain constant even though they appear different when seen from a different perspective. (This change of viewpoints is the subject of projective geometry, discussed in chapter 4).

The magic bubble encapsulating the child slowly expands through interaction with others. While very young children still have difficulty conceptualizing thoughts and feelings different from their own, they begin to recognize similarities.

A toddler can view a crying newcomer to his playgroup with real understanding: "He is crying because he misses his mummy." One such toddler was seen rushing to his cubby to retrieve his pacifier to give to the sobbing child. He was convinced that whatever comforted him would comfort the other child, too.

The loosening of egocentric thought slowly permits beginning social interaction in the use of blocks. Children usually make their first buildings in solitary splendor, and the accidental bumping of two bodies, both on their own building, may lead to the joining of the two. It may be as simple as connecting two sets of tracks, but this is the next step in socialization. The accidental associating with another child opens a new vista. Each child alone may have quickly lost interest in block building, but together they continue to use and build the tracks. The addition of other ideas increases interest and often makes children more aware of what they are doing. Here is an example from *Before Books*:

Cooperation and acceptance of each other's input occurs when children have an atmosphere in which they can experiment.

> Railroad tracks are becoming the dominant interest of the group, and more concentrated work is done in this occupation at present than in any other. There is much enjoyment in cooperation and though building may begin alone, tracks are usually connected with each other. On Monday, Craig made the usual type of track. When Craig began to run a train near this part of the track, Matthew said, "That's the Subway, wait, it isn't finished yet, I'm going to make it dark." Then he started to lay blocks on top. The first size he tried was too short. He recognized this at once, went for a larger size, and put one on, when Craig interfered, saying, "That's not right, you must make it higher so that cars can go in it." Matthew accepted this and they made the sides higher and added a roof. The other part of the track became a trolley track, and large car barn was added. (Pratt & Stanton 1926, 30–31)

Harmonious cooperation can soon break down, however, when the desires of the two playmates conflict. When two children have their hearts set on playing with the same truck, for example, a fight is sure to erupt. At this age it is rather futile to try to teach children the virtues of taking turns or sharing. Even though children might follow the adults' suggestions because of their need to be loved by them, no real learning results. It might be possible, however, to begin helping children to grasp how another person feels. "David wants his truck very badly. Remember how you felt when you wanted that puzzle all by yourself?" Relating David's feelings to his own experience makes these feelings more real to a child. Here are the beginnings of empathy (Hendrick 1996).

Egocentricity decreases also through children's identification with a beloved teacher.

> A little girl complained because her teacher would always sit next to Maria's bed rather than her own at naptime. The teacher

explained, "Maria needs it." "Oh," said the child and after lunch placed a chair for the teacher next to Maria's cot.

Acceptance of individual differences is facilitated by cooperative block play. Block play stimulates appreciation of the ideas of others, even though these ideas may be different or even conflict with one's own. Eventually true social give-and-take can develop. Grasping and accepting individual differences is a major lifelong task of social studies.

Group living

The beginning acceptance of classmates as distinct individuals would be difficult without verbal communication. Language is used as a tool to assist in making social contact. At the same time, working with others precipitates a powerful surge in the richness and complexity of language use.

Children younger than 3 often do not yet think in words, although they understand and can use language. Piaget (1926) suggested two classes of speech, egocentric speech and socialized speech. Egocentric speech is not used for real communication. In fact, two children can maintain what Piaget calls a "collective monologue." They may sit side by side, pause while the other talks, then continue their own train of thought, which has nothing to do with what the other child was talking about. Cooperation, however, soon develops, as illustrated by Pratt and Stanton.

> The new feature in block building this week has been the fine cooperation displayed by children working together. Annie was the only child to build alone. When Mark began a track on Thursday, he said, "I want somebody to build with me," and Annie, putting away her own blocks, joined him. (1926, 97)

Here we see the moment when children seek others and no longer want to work alone. The need to socialize comes with growth. The ability to accept what another child suggests and not to rebel, even if things do not work out, is seen in this example.

> Mark foresaw the size of the block needed for a certain space and said, "We need a small block." Then he ran to the cupboard and, bringing the block back, fitted it into the space while Murray jumped up and down with excitement. Mark then returned for more blocks and came back with four, saying, "I'm taking four blocks." Murray did the same, only he said, "I'm taking three blocks," which was correct. The house being finished now, they ran to the cupboard for the fire engine. Each wanted an engine, but there was only one, so I suggested they use another kind of wagon as an engine. This turned out to be impractical, as each child who had made a wagon recognized his or hers as it came from the shelves, and called out that it was a milk wagon, or a lumber wagon. Mark and Murray then made efforts to adjust to the situation of only one engine. Mark said to Murray, who was holding it, "Would you just lend me your fire engine?" And then they said something about turns and carried it over and put it in the house. (Pratt & Stanton 1926, 97)

This cooperative venture did not end when there was only one fire engine. These children were able to find solutions to their problem, and what's more, they were able to understand a point of view other than their own; in Piaget's terms, they were *decentering*.

As block builders become more experienced, their social interaction becomes more complex as well. They argue, they give and follow suggestions, they offer ideas for the consideration of others. Language development, interpersonal understanding, and social development go hand in hand. The following example by Starks illustrates thinking, experimenting, group discussion, and exploration.

Carol, a rather mature five-year-old who rarely used blocks, began working one day on a tall building. The center part of one end was hollow and the other end had four floor levels. Soon she asked for string and

When children begin to be able to communicate their ideas to one another, they are capable of more planning and refinement of their jointly built structures.

proceeded to put several pieces, which she tied to a block. This she dropped into the open well of the building. By that time Jake and several other children had gathered around to see what she was doing. "It's an elevator," Carol announced happily. "See, the people are going up to the roof restaurant for lunch." She had trouble pulling the block up and down, however, and many suggestions were contributed by the interested spectators. With frank admiration, Tony (who was usually the instigator of elaborate ideas) announced, "I'll help you, Carol. I'll help you work it so that the people won't fall off." Interest in the elevator and its working and use led to a trip for part of the group to one of the older buildings in town where the cables and elevator could be watched through an open grille. Comments heard during the trip were put to use upon returning to the school: "It's a big cage with a building around it." "Big steel cables pull it up. There's a wheel—a pulley—that winds the cables and lifts that elevator." "You tell the man (operator) what floor you want and he stops the elevator at that floor. He makes the pulley stop winding the cable and that stops it." "An elevator is a cage that you ride up in. An escalator is stair steps that move." As a result of the trip, a small box was used as the elevator. Strings at each end led to the roof, where they were wound around a cylinder and could be rolled up or down as desired. Carol, her idea, and her construction became the center of a group varying in size from four to twelve during the period of at least two weeks. During the remainder of the year, others experimented with the idea with varying degrees of success. (Starks 1970)

This example shows how interaction with other preschoolers on a day-by-day basis has enabled children to accept and to use the ideas of others. Growing and learning in a good preschool environment develops children's sense of self and makes them valuable group members.

In a well-functioning group, peer leaders emerge. Such leaders are usually the ones who "have good ideas." Tony, in the above example, must have been such a leader. Like all genuine leaders, he was supportive of the group member (Carol) and helpful to her. Quite possibly it was this support that encouraged the interest and participation of other group members.

As children turn 6 it becomes important for them to try to function apart from the family. Success in creative work and the support of their peers becomes even more important.

Rubin describes friendship in the early childhood years as a "nonfamilial relationship likely to foster a feeling of belonging and a sense of identity" (1982, 236).

The inner world of children

A child's sense of self has a number of sources. "I'm OK," thinks the child, "because my parents think I am OK." But just as important as this parent-child relationship is the self-regard that results from the child's creative activity.

Blocks are a no-fail medium. Whatever the children construct serves as proof of their ability, their dexterity, and, eventually, their thought and imagination.

The placing together of several blocks and using them as a track is a feat of accomplishment. "Look what I did," children may say, not verbally, but in the way in which they look at the adult. Recognition of this success should be given, not necessarily in words, but at least with a returned look of pleasure or a nod of approval. Children at the youngest age need to have a feeling of competence. (White 1966)

White considers competence motivation a powerful driving force. He includes in his definition of competence such learned behaviors as manipulation, locomotion, language, the building of cognitive maps, skilled action, and the growth of effective social relations. Such acquisitions, according to White (1966), are made partly through exploratory and manipulative play.

The feeling of competence does not spring up overnight, however. Children are well aware of their helplessness and their dependence on adults. This is one of the reasons that so many of their play themes revolve around power. Parents, policemen, and teachers (some very mean teachers!) all exercise power. Since children cannot "think in their head," manipulative play permits them to examine roles and to think about what it feels like to have power. The externalization of inner thought helps children to "digest" experiences and come to terms with feelings. In the video *A Classroom with Blocks* (Berlfein 1987), a little boy is able to turn his pre-Halloween fears into a manageable, concrete "Spooky House." Similarly, block play, role playing, artwork, and, later, creative writing permit children to come to terms with other difficult experiences, such as hospitalization, accidents, or the birth of a new baby. The growth of competence acquired through a sense of mastery in play helps children to reduce the sense of helplessness that comes from being little in a big world. Gaining a

stronger sense of their own capability through play, they feel competent enough to overcome difficulties. At the same time, dramatic play serves as a medium for "thinking through action." It allows children to examine lives and social roles of other people. This is an important component of social studies.

Getting hold of the world

Piaget (1926) has shown that symbolic play moves through stages leading to increasing realism. Two- or 3-year-olds are quite content using a unit block as a car. By the time they reach 5 or 6, children insist on four wheels and a steering wheel for their vehicle. Representation through blocks allows children to examine the world around them. Beginning with their home or classroom, children can construct buildings that represent the geography of the school or of an entire city. Such mapmaking is shown vividly in the video *A Classroom with Blocks*. Depicting through construction engenders greater awareness of the environment. Children look at the whole scene, noticing details and questioning what they see. They become aware of people and what they do.

This awareness discloses new relationships, new consciousness of what makes things work and how people are related to things and to places. This social awakening can be the basis of the social studies program.

In the example cited, in which Carol struggled with the workings of an elevator, such a process of studying how things work is clearly illustrated. The group's interest in elevators was picked up by their teacher and led to field

When two or more children confer about how to represent and place the rooms of a house, parts of a city, or other components of a complex construction, each tries to communicate his or her own ideas and to comprehend what the other builder is suggesting.

study—a class trip. Block play leads to increased openness to the outside world. As children's interest in the world around them increases, trips will help to orient them directionally so that they can then take this knowledge back to the classroom.

Pratt and Stanton describe just such an occurrence in *Before Books* (1926):

The blocks have come into their own this week. The children have used them with keen interest and have made play schemes which have been enlarged from day to day. All but three children in the class have taken part in them, and other activities have been related to their block play. On Monday, I asked Fred what he was going to build when he returned to class, and he replied: "Wanamaker's." Meta said she would make "Seventh Avenue," and Florence decided to build her apartment house on Washington Square. Ready to work in the room, I asked Fred where he thought he had better make Wanamaker's and chose correctly the east side of the room. Meta made Seventh Avenue with blocks on the west side. She left spaces for the cross streets and drew them with chalk from Fourth to Twelfth Street. She had a very clear conception of the way streets ran. She built her apartment house on Fourth Street. I showed Florence where Seventh Avenue and Eighth Street were, and she built her apartment on the next street to the south. A large round cylinder block placed in a square puzzled me, but Florence informed me that it was the boiler in the cellar and held the hot water that heated the building. She made Washington Square next. Dolls were seated on benches. Paper scratched over with green crayon represented the grass. Sonia made the Woolworth Tower at the extreme south end of the room. Fred worked steadily on Wanamaker's. The only things within the very large square which represented the store were the elevator and some "offices." It is interesting to note that what Fred has seen chiefly in watching the elevator was the great rod that pushed it up. He represented this by a very long block, which he stood upright. Thumbtacks on blocks represented the elevator lights which he had watched. He made the door by which he had entered in exactly the correct location, the southeast corner, and drew marks on the floor to represent our class going in. Celia built the school and Alan, his own house. (p. 15)

The vitality of a social studies program and its organic connection with literacy skills are described by Antin (1952).

An exciting study of food coming into our city by trains and barges, over bridges and through tunnels, also includes activities which answer the needs of children who are still playing out home and family relationships. For who ever heard of a city where there are no houses for people to live in? Where do the boat and train men go at the end of a day's work? How can people live without department stores? Or grocery stores, jewelry shops, restaurants, garages, banks, playgrounds, beauty parlors? Buses are needed and sight-seeing boats. The block-city needs people, and people properly dressed. Plasticine comes to the rescue, and bits of material, paper, crayons, scissors, and paste. Docks and trains need number signs. Buildings, streets, boats, businesses have names. Traffic signs and danger signals are needed. Money, with the number quantity written on it, becomes necessary. What goes on here? John's railroad tracks are crowding out streets for taxis and trucks! And freight coming into our city must be shipped from all over the country by train. When we were down by the markets, how did we see our city work it out? Hundreds of trucks and cars fill the streets and yet the trains came in and went out! An overpass is needed! "Detour. Overpass being built." And so it goes. (p. 2)

This example shows the examination of geographic problems of the city is interwoven with economics. It shows how people live and work. These children would not have been able to learn about the complex interaction of geographic, social, and economic problems had their study been based on talk alone. Not even pictures, books, and audiovisual materials would have been sufficient to awaken the keen interest that grew through the hands-on activity with blocks. In the words of Lucy Sprague Mitchell ([1921] 1971) these youngsters were "getting hold of the world."

The acquisition of social knowledge

As Piaget (1969) points out, social knowledge differs from physical or logical-mathematical knowledge. Scientific facts can be discovered; they deal with principles that exist independent of people. Logical knowledge is derived from internal cognitive structures. Social knowledge is constructed by people. The words we use to label things, for instance, are arbitrary and thus, social knowledge.

Social knowledge in the elementary grades is transmitted not just in words but by deliberately exposing children to the wider world. Upper elementary-age children can learn about their society from community workers and from social institutions and complex operations of government on all levels. They are taught about the past, and they explore ways of living on distant continents.

All these understandings would be impossible, however, if children had not experienced, in their early years, intimate and extended relations with people, beginning at the home and proceeding to the school—with classmates, teachers, and other people in and around life in school.

This exposure can be further extended through trips. Trips can enable children to acquaint themselves with the entire school. On later trips, they can explore the immediate neighborhood and, in an ever-widening circle, the community and interesting neighboring areas with differing ways of life. These explorations will not only widen children's acquaintance with the school world, they also will bring spatial relationships into focus. Experiences then can be mulled over in the ways children need to grasp the world—through dramatic play, art, and importantly, through building with blocks.

Not all learning, however, is so neat and preplanned. Children experience the ways

Children's interest in and knowledge about the activities at the post office, airport, railroad yard, grocery store, or other sites—enhanced through reading about and visiting these places—are evident in their block play.

their society functions in many forms and from a variety of sources. Children receive information from their parents and family activities. They observe people's lives on television. Because their information-processing ability is not yet able to sort out this multitude of sometimes contradictory information, much of the school's task consists of providing a manageable way to examine the world and to grasp the way people live. Because children of this age are still under the influence of egocentrism, they cannot reverse—that is, they are unable to examine their internal representations directly and "think in their head."

The discussion below illustrates the confusion children experience when trying to sort out information they obtained from a variety of sources.

Barbara: I was wondering how trees ever came to be. You see, I was wondering how the Earth came to be—'cause I didn't live in the early days.

Bill: You see, the seeds blew, and other trees grew from the seeds.

Robert: How are seeds formed and how did the first trees ever come up?

Tom: I know there were wild trees.

Fran: It rained for thousands and thousands of years thousands of years ago.

Eve: I think God made the first seed.

Millie: Every year it rains, so new trees come out.

Ken: How would the seed bury itself?

Nate: Sometimes trees grow—no one planted the seeds.

Robert: But where did the first seed come from?

Ned: God made the seed, and he dropped it into the hole.

Tom: I have a very good idea. In the early days, the dinosaur dug the first hole.

Robert: In the beginning there was nothing, nothing. The Earth was just a glowing ball— when there were dinosaurs, there were trees.

Kris: 'Cause the dinosaurs ate the leaves of the trees.

Bart: Ned said God planted the first seed, but some people don't believe in God—what do they believe in?

Fay: When the dinosaurs lived, also turtles lived.

Eve: Turtles were living because in my book they were with the other fish, and maybe when God dropped seeds from the sky, Adam and Eve planted the seeds.

Bess: But how about those who don't believe in Adam and Eve? How could Adam open up his body, take out his chest, and give it to a girl?

Fran: I don't believe it's such a beautiful story.

Sue: God made the first man. I have a friend that doesn't believe in God. She said her parents made her.

Randy: What is God in the first place?

Nan: He's a spirit.

Millie: God made the first man. They were grownups—never babies. They had no clothes (no stores). So they had babies, and their children had children, and then they built houses and stores.

Tom: But how did they get stuff to build houses and stores?

Randy: They built houses out of wood—'cause they had trees. They didn't know from cement.

Bart: The first men really to live were cavemen, and these men were animals who turned into men.

Craig: They were apes.

Fran: People make their children in a way because they plan to have them.

Kris: I think the first people were Indians.

Ned: Indians were the second people; cavemen were the first.

Randy: In the Museum of Natural History there is the exhibit of Living Man—shows a road from the beginning to the start of man. So they did come from apes.

Millie: When I was there I saw all kinds of animals.

Bill: Maybe Columbus was the first one.

Tom: My mother read that Columbus really didn't discover New York.

Fran: When Columbus came, there were already Indians there, and they were nice.

Beth: God is like Eliahu—the spirit of love. Once on Passover he came and drank up all the wine.

Nan: When Columbus was on the boat— Queen said he said something they didn't like. They didn't like his thoughts. They put Columbus in jail for his thoughts.

Randy: They found a map, and now they are positive Columbus did not discover America first.

Barbara: My father said that Columbus came over in three boats.

Karl: I believe that the seeds were formed while the Earth was being formed.

This discussion followed a class trip to New York's Central Park. The teacher (who admirably refrained from interfering in the discussion) certainly had other goals in mind when she took these 6-year-olds on a trip.

It is not possible to structure a curriculum in a neat, sequential way, free from distracting and confusing influences. It is necessary, therefore, to build a conceptual support structure that will eventually allow an absorption and ordering of impressions and of information.

While blocks are not the only medium that supports activity-based thinking, they serve a very important role. In fact, blocks provide two kinds of exploration. The unit blocks designed by Caroline Pratt enable youngsters to examine the world from the outside. Hollow blocks, on the other hand, provide spaces and environments (rooms, stores, cars, etc.) that children can enter to engage in dramatic play.

The teacher's role

As in all other areas, teachers of young children must serve as facilitators to support social studies learning. The re-creation of the child's world requires that the teacher be close enough to assist, when necessary. Such assistance can consist of providing sufficient space for individuals or groups. Teachers provide accessories when appropriate and provide signs for more sophisticated builders. Teachers also provide more subtle stimulation by questioning, when appropriate. Questions can extend lagging activities. "Does your house need a garden?" "Would you like to decorate your building?" Questions also can clarify confusions and further the integration of knowledge. "How will people get into the building?" "How will they get to the top floor?" "How do cars get to the upper level of the garage?" "How do people know when it's safe to cross the street?" "How does the farmer let people know that he has a lot of apples to sell?" "Who looks after the animals in the zoo?" The teacher's responsibility to help children grow must extend to the growth that occurs through social interaction.

Teachers must be aware of children's ability to consider others and facilitate such development of empathy. They

Letting buildings stay up overnight, or even for several days, increases the value for children, especially as they become capable of building very complex and detailed structures.

also must stay abreast of the developing group forces, use within-group leadership, and prevent scapegoating and rejection of individuals.

As children become more experienced and mature, teachers also can pick up on their interest by providing pictures, supplying books, and taking appropriate trips.

After a strenuous building session, young children often request that their building be left standing. However, children 4 and younger seldom carry their interest over from one day to the next. Moreover, the leftover building will take up space and deplete the block supply that could be available for new construction.

Beginning with kindergarten, block-building projects become more and more complex. These more detailed buildings usually require more time to build and may need more than one session to build and to use. Letting buildings stay up overnight and possibly for several days increases the value of the activity to children. It might take all the allotted time to build a swimming pool, color a paper to indicate the water, construct a diving board, and put people in and around it. *Where is the time to use it? Where is the time to involve others in the building? Where is the time to tell others about the building?* Children need to have time to dramatize and to include other members of the group in the activity. The cooperation that went into the construction of the building and the pride in the construction are just part of the whole. Children's need to use the building is as great as their need to make it. Teachers have to be aware of this when they plan the time and the space for their block corners.

In the primary grades, children can begin mapmaking with blocks. Such projects might take an extended period of time and require a great deal of investigation and clarification. Such three-dimensional maps should deal with location accessible to the class.

The video *A Classroom with Blocks* shows an extended project by third-graders engaged in making a map of their school. Their map covers the entire classroom. Since blocks are three-dimensional, mapping with blocks permits the construction of scale-model building. This type of mapping is less abstract and therefore more meaningful, even for elementary-age children, than the usual wall maps and globes used for geography classes. The teacher's role here was to stimulate the project, provide environment and material, and, most important, provide encouragement and support.

The aim of teachers in block building, as in all other areas, is to facilitate the integration of knowledge through experience-based activities.

References

Antin, C. *Blocks in the curriculum.* 1952. New York: Early Childhood Education Council of New York City.

Berlfein, J., prod. 1987. *A classroom with blocks.* Washington, DC: NAEYC. Videocassette.

Hendrick, J. 1996. *The whole child.* 6th ed. New York: Merrill/Macmillan.

Mahler, M.S. 1968. *On human symbiosis and the vicissitudes of individuation.* New York: International University Press.

Mitchell, L.S. [1921] 1971. *Young geographers.* New York: John Day; New York: Agathon.

Piaget, J. 1926. *The language and thought of the child.* New York: Harcourt Brace and World.

Piaget, J. 1969. *Science of education and the psychology of the child.* New York: Viking.

Pratt, C., & J. Stanton. 1926. *Before books.* New York: Adelphi.

Rubin, Z. 1982. "What is a friend?" In *Readings in a developmental psychology,* ed. J.K. Gardener. Boston: Little Brown.

Starks, E.B. 1970. *Blockbuilding.* Washington, DC: American Association of Elementary-Kindergarten-Nursery Educators.

White, R.W. 1966. Competence and the psychosexual stages of development. In *The causes of behavior,* eds. J.F. Rosenblith & W. Allinsmith. Boston: Allyn & Bacon.

6

Dramatic Play: The Experience of Block Building

Harriet K. Cuffaro

One of the most profound means available to children for constructing and reconstructing, formulating and reformulating knowledge is through play. It is a means for synthesis and integration in that it brings together the child's concept of reality with the inner world of fantasies and feelings. Play may be seen as the child's substitute for adult musing, contemplation, hypothesizing, meandering among ideas and experiences. Play is the visible language of childhood wherein we see and hear the total child functioning, revealing individual concerns, conflicts, information and misinformation, ambivalences, wishes, hopes, pleasures, and questions. Where the adult discusses an experience and via words—thought or spoken—explores nuances, connections, and possible meanings, the child requires the context of activity for such probing and exploration.

Verbal thinking can hardly yet be *sustained in its own right*, in earlier years. It draws its vitality from the actual problems of concrete understanding and of manipulation in which it takes its rise and solution of which it furthers. (Isaacs 1966, 84–85)

Play encompasses an almost infinite variety of activities. The growing literature on play, aside from exploring its variety and meaning, also has indicated how difficult it is to capture this activity of childhood in definition. What follows is not a definition of play but rather a statement of elements that I deem necessary to its consideration.

Two things seem to be essential: activity and self-direction. Activity is defined here not only as motion—as in walking, running, and reaching—but also as the activity, the engagement, of the senses. Self-direction explains itself; the direction of the activity is determined by the child. What starts play, how it proceeds, where it leads, when it stops, what it includes or excludes, what it ignores or connects to—these are choices made by the child consciously or unconsciously. Many factors influence the child's selection. Important among them is the level of development, which determines functioning ability; the degree of interest, curiosity, and knowledge invested; the individual's use of affect—that uniquely personal conglomerate of feelings and fantasies born of interaction with the world of people and things.

Many kinds of play include these two elements. The chapter headings in Lowenfeld's *Play in Childhood* (1967) reveal not only an interesting classification of play activities but also the varying functions of play—for example, "Play as Bodily Activity," "Play as Repetition of Experience," "Play as the Demonstration of Phantasy," "Play as Realisation of Environment," and "Play as Preparation for Life." Other writers may use such phrases as *imaginative play* and *imitative play*. My focus is on yet another label for play, one that includes aspects of all the classifications stated above: *dramatic play*.

The word *drama* evokes visions of theater. The child's dramatic play and the world of theater may find alliance and provoke comparison. Both deal with a blending of reality, fantasy, and imagination—elements that are used personally and uniquely, unpressured by time and space. In each, a world is selectively created from aspects of reality, with feelings and wishes blended through imagination to reflect a particular view, a personal understanding. To carry the analogy further, in dramatic play the script is created out of the child's totality of experience; the cast is the child performing as self and also as other selves, reflecting roles being imitated, rehearsed, or projected. Dramatic play is a play always in rehearsal, an ongoing production. What is understood, explored, initiated, reconstructed, synthesized moves into the script, thereby altering it while in production.

Dramatic play may occur in many settings, engaging a child alone or with others, with or without props.

Play must be seen as the child's substitute for adult musing, contemplation, hypothesizing, meandering among ideas and experiences.

We see it in the child sitting alone, "driving a bus"; in a group of children sitting in a schoolyard "on a picnic in the park"; in a serious little group engrossed in the drama of "a sick baby attended by a doctor"; in two children involved in "a primeval battle" between two clay dinosaurs they have molded; in the busy activity of a child "collecting garbage on a truck from house to house" in a city block scheme. Each of these situations has its own possibilities, defined by the limitations and potential of the particular medium being used, by the setting, and by the child.

In narrowing the focus of investigation to the dramatic play that may occur in relation to block building in a *group setting*, it would be helpful to explore not only the play of the child but also the nature of the medium and how it affects and influences activity.

Throughout this chapter, the blocks referred to are the unit blocks for indoor use designed by Caroline Pratt (1948). They do not bear her name but are sold under various trademarks. When reference is made to the larger hollow blocks, it will be so specified.

Block building and dramatic play

I would broadly define dramatic play with blocks as the self-directed activity that occurs between a child and the structure created by the child and wherein a transactional relationship exists between subject and object. The child creates an object—the structure—and endows it in imagination with representations and reflections of her or his experiences, fantasies, information. The structure is then a tangible representation to the child of personal ideas and feelings and, in this symbolic form, then serves as a stimulus for expanding activity and imaginings. It becomes, for the child, a tangible point of reference for questioning and contemplation, activities that would be difficult without connection with the concrete. As the child explores reality and as ideas are expanded, this flow of thoughts and feelings is reflected in the changes the child makes in the structure. For example, amendments to a building, alterations, and added details may be seen as the child's recording of the development of an idea. This recording then may serve as a means for review and further examination when the structure is used.

Just as building structures may follow a developmental progression, as was vividly and richly documented by Harriet Johnson's *The Art of Block Building* ([1933] 1966, or this volume, chapter 2), so does the play connected with it. Generally, play seems to move in stages, from solitary play, in which there are brief encounters with others; to play of a more associative nature in which one or two children work loosely connected to other groups of children; to play that is in cooperation with others and is more sustained, often planned, and extends over a longer period of time.

No matter in which of these stages the child might be, using blocks for dramatic play requires the child to (1) create the context for play rather than finding it already prepared; (2) deal with reality and scale in translating ideas to the medium; and (3) gradually step outside of self to a symbolized self in play (these three tasks will be discussed in greater detail). It is usually in the cooperative play of 5-year-olds, especially those who have had

In the block area, children create the context for dramatic play, somewhat as if they were creating the theater set in which a play is to unfold.

the opportunity to use blocks freely and with sufficient time to explore ideas, that many of these characteristics will appear most clearly. By this age the child's experiences in the social and physical world have helped to expand perspective and knowledge. By age 5, children's horizons have extended beyond the immediacy of family, and they are ready to exercise this understanding. (While mentioning a specific age, I simultaneously add the caution that such usage is an approximation because many factors—culture, quality of previous experience, development, maturation, socioeconomic setting—influence chronology. Also to be considered is that children function on various levels of development, incorporating into the present moment elements of the past while also stretching toward the future.)

Creating the context for play

The general setting for dramatic play is created by the adult in the allocation of space, the number and variety of blocks provided, and the addition of supplementary materials such as rubber or wooden people and animals, cars, planes, boats, cloth, paper, string, colored cubes, containers, and sticks. The space should be adequate and not hampered by being a passageway for traffic or encumbered by tables and other furniture.

In a sense, a theater with a bare stage has been made ready with props available for creating the set. In a housekeeping area the child *finds* the set of refrigerator, stove, sink, bed, table, chairs, and other props. In the block area the child must *create* the set or context for the play that will unfold. In the former instance, the child enacts a role in a setting established by others; in the latter, the child not only enacts a role but also is called upon to design and produce the setting. Blocks do not make a statement in themselves other than conveying a feeling of harmony and durability. This is in contrast to a stove or sink in the housekeeping area that is clearly defined. Of course, the child is free to imagine the stove to be a boat by ignoring its detail. In such an instance, it would seem that the child is not engaged with the stove itself; it becomes merely a stepping stone for the flow of ideas. Building one's own stove through the realization of an idea in tangible form is an act of creation.

The block, in having no predetermined identity other than its physical state of smoothness, hardness, and shape, is a blank on which or with which the child makes his or her impact. Children must *do* and *make* in order for play to commence. The younger the child, the greater is the emphasis on the *doing* and on self-participation. Later the *making—creating*—is added to action. For example, a young 3-year-old may take a block and push it across the floor, tooting, puffing, swaying like a boat. Child, block, and boat are fused into a oneness that is generalized, global. In this younger stage, it is the *feel* of the boat—the being/imagining of boatness—that is externalized in physical expression. As play evolves, the details of reality and information are added, and some separation begins to occur between self and object. It is no longer sufficient to endow the object through sound and motion and to imagine that it is a boat. It has to take form and must be physically endowed as a boat. Size and shape of blocks take on new importance as the child moves to grouping, selecting, and arranging blocks to create the boat. Some of that earlier *feel* is now *out* of self and passed on to the details of the object.

Reality and scale in translation of idea to medium

No matter how a structure is started—whether a child comes to the block shelf ready to build a house or whether the structure becomes a house as blocks are handled—the child's task is to translate an idea into actuality. The house may represent the conglomerate of houses known; it may be a selection of images from those features that have the most meaning for the child. The representation will include the child's information about houses and the child's feelings about them. It may be a house consisting solely of a kitchen, or one with rooms for people and animals, or a barricaded building without windows or doors. Whatever the structure becomes, the task of the child is to translate an internalized idea or concept into an externalized representation. In the translation of images, the child must deal structurally with the question of relationships—balance, fit, proportion, order. In the act of symbolizing, the child is assisted by the unitary, harmonious nature of blocks. In their scaled order, blocks promote proportion and relationships that may support the child's task of connecting fragments of images and feelings toward a combined whole, a synthesis. Also, the fact that blocks cannot be altered, bent, or folded requires that the child adapt to the demands of that reality.

The unyielding, durable nature of the material and its characteristics of harmony and scale are part of the world of reality, and it is into that real world that children seek to bring their images. I recall the dilemma of a child working out a turn on his two-way elevated highway. He was distressed by the lack of smoothness in his incline and by the turn itself. These were some of his thoughts as he accompanied action with words:

"If you have a bump when you turn, you could have an accident; if I don't turn here, my highway can't go anywhere, only into that building, and a highway doesn't go *into* buildings; that kind of block doesn't fit, it's too big for the way my highway grows; it has to be bigger here (width) when it goes around, 'cause how will the other car (coming from the opposite direction) know where its place is to be safe?"

He finally worked it out by driving a car back and forth, looking, trying, changing blocks, and in a triumphant moment, when all the trying jelled, he exclaimed, "Wait, wait! I know!" He altered the incline of the ramp leading to the curve, and everything literally fell into place. Process and product were intertwined as the child evoked from self the representation to be created.

Distancing: From self to symbolic self and other symbolizations

In the process of distancing, the child separates from self that which is within the self. As mentioned earlier, when the very young child is exploring a boat, it may be done with any object that can be moved. In such doing, there is a flow between child and object as they mesh together. Gradually, and over an extended period of time and experiences, the child moves in dramatic play to a more objective directing of objects and props which support the play. A series of examples may serve to illustrate this evolution.

1. A young 4-year-old builds a simple block structure called a "house" and plays the role of mother to a baby doll. Another child joins the play and becomes the pet kitten. Yet another child joins the group and becomes the big brother. Although the group has enlarged, the structure may remain the same. Possibly an enclosure may be added to house the 4-year-old, who is curled into a ball and meowing. If needed, the other children may stretch out on the floor near the building.

2. With the same group toward the end of the year, we may find the same child once again building a house. Now the house may be more complex, with partitions creating rooms rather than the previous suggestion of a room. We again find the doll on the bed, and next to it the big brother, who this time is not a child but a rubber or wooden figure. The kitten, still meowing and purring, lies in a more elaborate environment, with a bowl for milk, a pillow, a blanket, and a "decoration" for play.

3. And yet another example, as our small group is now 5-year-olds in the spring of the following year. I recall a specific house, complete with kitchen, bedrooms, living room, and many bathrooms. Each of the rooms was furnished in great detail. Small drawings were pasted on the walls as framed pictures. The kitchen's stove, refrigerator, and sink, built of unit blocks and squares, had paper taped on them to indicate the jets, faucets, and knobs. In the house lived a family of rubber people—a mother, a father, two sisters, and a baby brother.

These three examples illustrate some progressive stages in the development of dramatic play with blocks: increasing attention given to the details of reality and the question of scale, which were discussed in the preceding section, and gradual movement from involvement in play via direct participation to participation through a symbolized self represented by a rubber or wooden figure, which will now be explored.

A lessening of egocentricity is one of the necessary steps in cognitive development, which has as a goal the ability to think logically, analytically, and objectively. Objectivity requires distance from self and the ability to comprehend frames of reference other than one's own. This cannot occur without the existence of opportunities that reveal alternatives or the feeling of discordance or conflict that may grow out of situations in which basic premises are shaken. Whenever a child takes yet another step in linking to the world of reality, such situations and opportunities become available. They are also present in the dramatic play accompanying block building because children in play are re-creating their experiences and questions of the moment. As reality sharpens and takes more distinct form, it becomes more tangible. It separates from the global, and thus the child is better able to examine, experiment with, and begin to direct that which has been differentiated. The role being played may take on shading

and variation. It would seem that as form becomes more definite, it also grows in depth, as it is reinforced and rooted with the addition of detail and by conforming to the proportions and relationships found in reality.

The child begins a similar process in defining self in relation to the social world. In the three examples given in this section, we see how the structure of dramatic play may supply the child with situations and opportunities in which to examine and rehearse the processes of differentiation and individuation and their results. The child's *direct participation through self* in the first and second examples is relinquished in the third example to a symbolized self onto whom feelings and actions are *projected*. The child may stand outside of self for limited periods of time and function as if someone else, and enact a role in adherence to her or his understanding of this other role. In the projection onto a symbolized self or selves, the child is able to assume a *variety* of roles in rehearsal and imitation, to experiment with them without the pressure of time or consequences. Just as the child's knowledge of physical reality moves from the global to the specific and the child is thus able to examine, experiment with, and direct that which has taken form, so it is in the realm of people and feelings. Through play, the child has an opportunity to externalize a variety of emotions—amorphous, potent, ambivalent—and thus make them available for examination and understanding. Also externalized is the child's understanding of relationships and roles, knowledge that may be difficult to accept because it conflicts with wishes and desires, is confusing, or is simply incomprehensible. In play, the child takes information and misinformation and tests it against reality.

> Play is not only the means by which the child comes to discover the world; it is supremely the activity which brings him psychic equilibrium in the early years. In his play activities, the child externalizes and works out to some measure of harmony all the different trends of his internal psychic life . . . And gradually he learns to relate his deepest and most primitive phantasies to the ordered world of real relations. (Isaacs 1972, 425)

As some of these remarks are related to dramatic play in general, I would like to stress an essential difference involved when the dramatic play is connected to block building. Once the child moves into using a symbolic self (i.e., the rubber or wooden figures), it becomes possible for the child to experiment with more roles. For example, in directing the activities of four rubber or wooden figures in a setting that she or he has created, a child may alternately be mother, baby, father, and teacher. Not only is each *role* tested but also the *relationships* existing among the various roles.

Finally, the process of building is in itself an act of distancing as the child externalizes thoughts and feelings. There are times in the externalization when the child creates a structure that is representative, but there are also times when the child engages in building activities that are exploratory and not necessarily goal directed. If our attention is caught only by the recognizable, then we may miss the steps leading to it. The seemingly aimless building in which a child may engage is an important step in the total process of symbol-ization. The importance of this step may be understood if we compare it to the time needed "to fool around," "to toy with" an idea before it begins to take shape and find direction. There are many steps to be taken as the child externalizes thoughts and feelings. As Lowenfeld says,

> Play is in a sense artistic creation; each piece of play of this kind is a new creation, and its creation is intimately connected with the development of thought, for until a concept has been expressed, or an experience externalized, it cannot give place to another thought. (1967, 161)

Group setting

In the classroom, block building and the accompanying dramatic play take place in a group setting—a fact that has important implications not only for the social development of the child but also for cognitive and emotional development. A child working alone with blocks at home is still bringing to the building situation the elements mentioned earlier: creating context for play, dealing with reality and scale in the translation of ideas, and moving to a symbolized self in play. What ultimately would be missing if building were to continue as solitary play would be the impact and enrichment, the testing of one's knowledge and feelings, that may occur in interaction with the reality and feelings of others.

In the preceding section, three examples were given that illustrated the development of play around the central theme of *home*, and certain progressions were noted. In examining the social aspects of this play, we should not

Blocks permit choices in the social context: the child may build alone and ignore others; build alone and work with others; build as part of a small group; or, along with the other children, accept a common challenge.

infer that in such progressions the number of children working together diminishes as surrogate figures take their place. On the contrary, social interaction is increased and expanded, as block play begins to take on a community aspect. For example, concerning distancing and the movement from direct participation to symbolic representation, the child's focus in the first anecdote is on the personal, immediate world she has created, but in the last example, the child has moved outward from the personal base of her block home to interact with all the possibilities offered by the other children. In the last of the three illustrations, other structures found in the same block scheme were a *school* (which her children attended); a *supermarket* (where she purchased her groceries—usually milk,

bread, ice cream, and candy); a *fire department* (from which workers came to put out a fire in her house—a fire she refused to have, so they went to another, more obliging home); a *playground* (which was used by the school and to which she took her children, who were either very compliant or extraordinarily disobedient and were accordingly rewarded or punished); a *hospital* (which she visited once because her baby had "a boiling fever"); a *department of sanitation* (she did not visit the incinerator plant, but she dutifully complied with the directions of the garbage collectors); and a *police station* (her only contact with the police was to thank them for returning her lost children).

Certain things become apparent in the brief parenthetical remarks concerning the nature of this child's interaction with the other children. Each child in that block scheme had created not only a structure but also a set of rules that governed behavior and was appropriate to the role being played. In each encounter she had to deal not only with her rules but also with the rules of others, and there were instances when she found encounters with these other realities difficult to accept. In addition, she was able to observe styles of functioning that differed from her own. She observed other interpretations of parental roles as other mothers and fathers took their children to the park and to school. Of great importance was that she could regulate the degree of her participation. Without undue pressure she could select those realities with which she could contend. She could engage in a variety of activities, using the variety of identities within herself by directing the behavior of mother, father, baby, and other surrogate figures in her symbolic family.

Blocks permit children choices in the social context: one may build alone and ignore others; build alone and work with others; build as part of a small group within a larger group; or, along with the other children, accept a common challenge. The variations are many. The material accommodates not only the sequence of social development but also the moods and needs of the moment.

Educational implications

This second part addresses the application of the ideas presented. Formulas and activities will not be offered; teachers must find the practices that are compatible with their values and that seem appropriate for the children with whom they are working. What will be presented are some underlying criteria for teachers to consider and a clearer definition of the opportunities offered.

Symbolization

It is a long road from cooing and babbling to speaking in coherent sentences, from an unplanned line on paper to the intentional writing of a word that can be read and understood. There are many steps to be taken on these roads, many pauses, many detours. The child needs time to try and to test skills and opportunities to use symbols in self-directed activities in order to get the *feel* of the pro-

cess. The child must have the chance to function on an *as if* level, to understand that one thing may stand for another. Dramatic play stemming from block building is a situation in which the child's symbolic activities grow out of the core of the child's living and, consequently, are relevant and meaningful to the child. In the externalization of images and feelings, both in actual building and in dramatic play, the child is engaged actively, functioning as an integrated self using body, feelings, senses, and thought. Within such opportunities, children work themselves into the symbolic process with interest and a self-regulated tempo. In the doing, the child not only learns how to do but also prepares for what will ultimately lead to the ability to work with abstract ideas, letters, and numbers.

As children move into sign-level representations, that is, into the realm of letters, numbers, punctuation marks, and mathematical notations, they need the time and the opportunities for experimentation and testing. Once again, children must get the *feel* of the process and begin to understand an order that they have not created but must accept. Often children may find entrance to this level of representation by giving birth to their own system, but for such a system to be born, a need to communicate must exist. Such openings occur naturally in block building: scribbles on a piece of paper pasted on a road to indicate *warning;* arrows giving directions; colored cubes indicating traffic lights; a drawing of a flower to indicate a florist's shop; colored designs taped on a block house to indicate the address. From these beginnings grows the understanding that leads to the labels seen so frequently in block schemes: *STOP, Danger,*

84

Gas station, Go slow, Don't knock my building down. These messages, dictated to teachers, are part of the experimentation begun in the simple scribbles drawn in imitation of the codes of the adult world.

The need for these symbols grows out of the child's activities, thus imbuing the symbols with personal meaning and significance. At first these personal symbols may have meaning only for the child, but as activity occurs in a group context, the child is moved toward using and developing signs that may be understood by others. This evolution also may be extended to the communication involved in discussions and conversation that grow out of the happenings in a block scheme. Children have an opportunity to move from an egocentric to a sociocentric perspective as they exchange ideas, solve problems jointly, pose questions for each other, and begin to see how the world looks from the vantage point of another. In all these activities, children's block structures become a concrete base to which they may return for reference. Obviously, there are many opportunities offered in block building and dramatic play to create, use, and function within the symbolic realm. Such activi-

Block play gives children the impetus to exchange ideas, solve problems jointly, pose questions for each other, and begin to see how the world looks from the vantage point of another.

ties, growing out of the interests of the child, are an important phase in the development and refinement of the symbolic process.

Before proceeding to the next section, I would like to consider one further point in relation to the child's distancing through a symbolized self. As in other areas of development, when a child moves into a new stage, this does not mean that arrival signals new behavior that makes a clean break with the old. There is unevenness in behavior, a turning back at times to earlier modes of response. This becomes evident in dramatic play with blocks. For example, children who are perfectly able to use surrogate figures to represent self/selves in play with satisfaction and concentration may still need and use opportunities for more direct participation with structures they have created.

Hollow blocks, also designed by Caroline Pratt, are much larger than the indoor unit blocks and are more appropriately scaled for use by the child directly and not through a surrogate figure. These hollow blocks are most often used outdoors, and it is here that we may see some of the same dramatic play from the classroom block scheme transferred to the outdoors. The group that has built a space center in the classroom—complete with launching pad, gantry, controls, with rubber or wooden astronauts launched into space—may build outdoors a larger space capsule from which the children themselves may zoom off into space to find treasures and adventure in the unknown.

I recall, as a further example, a mixed-age group of 4- through 6-year-olds who had built a block city. One of the buildings was a post office. The teacher took the group for several trips to a post office to add to their information. Following these experiences the children returned to their block city post office with more understanding and details to be included, yet their teacher sensed that they needed more direct reliving of their experiences. In this instance, the distancing through a surrogate figure removed them too far from the feel of what they were exploring. What developed was an abandoning for a while of the smaller, indoor blocks and a turning to the indoor use of hollow blocks, with which the children built a functioning post office that serviced several classrooms. Letters were written, notes delivered, and packages mailed in a week of highly satisfying and exciting learning. Children need opportunities for both types of experiences as they shuttle back and forth between stages of symbolization.

Connecting self and knowledge

Earlier I proposed that play may be viewed as the child's substitute for adult reflection, musing, and hypothesizing. Play is the child's way of bringing things together to find their relationship and connections while seeking clarification and understanding. The young child's task is to sort, order, and synthesize the information gathered from growing experiences in and interaction with the social and physical world. Information gathered in fragmented fashion is bent and turned to fit into the familiar. In some instances, like the peg that is too big for the hole, all the bends and turns do not make things fit, and so the child must seek further in order to connect the parts and pieces. The same task confronts the child in terms of self—putting together feelings, fantasies, and reality. The child's understanding of self and the child's understanding of the world grow together and are intertwined.

In the joint activities of block building and dramatic play, the child is able to make certain connections: (1) between self and knowledge, by filtering new knowns through the backlog of experience; and (2) within self, through the imaginative activities that help to bring together feelings, fantasies, and reality. In this latter synthesis the child combines the inner life of unconscious fantasy and the more accessible realm of known feelings with reality. It is only for the purpose of examination that I make this separation, for within the person the two are blended and interwoven. There are times when one part may predominate, subordinating the other, but invariably there is an interweaving that binds them together. It is in acts of imagination that a person is able to bring together, in working harmony, reality and fantasy thinking. Imagination includes reality because they are related, just as fantasy includes desires and drives because of their relationship.

The child has the opportunity to bring together reality and fantasy thinking in the imaginative activities of block building and dramatic play. The experiences of both realms are brought together in imagination and expressed in activity. As the child works at achieving a balance between fantasy and reality, play often reflects the greater weight of one or the other. What is important in the activities of building and the play stemming from it is that the child is offered a *vehicle* for the act of balancing reality and fantasy. Too often the world of feelings, dreams, and wishes is ignored by educators, which unfortunately leads to learning situations in which the child is only partially present, for what has been canceled is the engagement of the child's most personal self and her or his continuity.

If we value integration of self and responding to the whole child in a learning situation, then block building combined with dramatic play offers such opportunities for the teacher, just as these activities offer the child the opportunity to integrate information in the act of re-experiencing it. The re-experiencing becomes in itself an experience from which new connections may grow as the subjective and objective are intertwined, for in the doing the child wisely does not separate the cognitive and affective domains.

Expanding thinking style

From a 1964 Conference on Cognitive Studies and Curriculum Development held in the United States, I would like to present two remarks made by Piaget:

The principal goal of education is to create men who are capable of doing new things, not simply of repeating what other generations have done—men who are creative, inventive, and discoverers. The second goal of education is to form minds which can be critical, can verify, and not accept everything they are offered. (in Ripple & Rockcastle 1964, 5)

The question comes up whether to teach the structure, or to present the child with situations where he is active and creates the structures himself. . . . The goal in education is not to increase the amount of knowledge, but to create the possibilities for the child to invent and discover. When we teach too fast, we keep the child from inventing and discovering himself. . . . Teaching means creating situations where structures can be discovered; it does not mean transmitting structures which may be assimilated at nothing other than a verbal level. (in Ripple & Rockcastle 1964, 3)

If thinking is to avoid stereotypic formulas, be critical and analytic in nature, and honor the originality and independence of the thinker, then the learning situations created to foster its development must model the very charac-

In the imaginative activities of block building and dramatic play, the child has the opportunity to bring together reality and fantasy thinking.

teristics to be promoted. The "possibilities for the child to invent and discover" will certainly not arise in classrooms that inflexibly dictate the activities of the child, request regurgitation of facts, limit the style of response, and offer scant opportunity for the child's interaction and synthesis.

Learning situations must be sufficiently flexible and open ended to permit the child scope in both thinking and activity. Such environments have been described in the wealth of books and articles on open education. Similar themes were examined and explored in great depth in the writings of John Dewey and other proponents of progressive education. Whatever the source, those learning situations that emphasize flexibility and open endedness—viewed not as ends in themselves but as consciously held values that help promote independence, initiative, and inventiveness on the part of the learner—also tend to encourage divergence, experimentation, and analysis in thinking. Such an approach honors nuance, alternatives, choice, variety, doubt, and freedom. This is the antithesis of a world of closure which has found all the right answers and in which there are few options, consequently leaving little, if any, room for self-discovery.

In block building and dramatic play, children not only have opportunities for self-discovery but also the time and place where they may exercise the type of open thinking that has been discussed. To exercise choice is an ever-present option: what structure to build, which role to play, how shall it be portrayed, which detail to add, which image to select, which emotion to display, which interaction is preferred. An awareness of alternatives exists not only because play extends over a period of time, which in itself creates opportunities for choices, but also because in the group context, a variety of interpretations becomes evident in interaction.

The *as if* nature of dramatic play is akin to the hypothetical moment. Without the pressures of time and consequence or a demanding reality, the child has the opportunity to toy with ideas and, in such self-directed playfulness, to discover the new and original. Finally, in creating an *as if* situation, the child adheres behaviorally to the hypothetical premises stated and maintains a certain order to be followed within the social context of the group. This development in dramatic play might be seen as a precursor of group games, in which the child identifies with the group and adheres to its rules.

The role of the teacher

In connection with block building and dramatic play, what might be the role of the teacher? Thus far, emphasis has centered on the child's role in self-directed learning and the opportunities that arise from use of the material and the activities that complement it. Earlier I stated that it is the teacher who allocates space, quantity and variety of blocks, and supplementary materials. To this may be added (1) the creation of the social atmosphere in which learning and interaction occur, and (2) the adult's role as guide or catalyst in the learning situations that arise or are provided.

What does it mean specifically to act as guide, catalyst, and—to add another element—synthesizer? Examples may serve to illustrate these roles:

1. In a block scheme, a boy had built a fish store, which he stocked by going fishing in the river (two blue lines, painted on the floor, across the width of the room, which separated city from country). A girl went to his store to buy fish for her family and was told that the store was closed. Every time she went to his store, he closed it. Finally, in great irritation, she yelled at him, "You can't do that. A store has to sell—that's what it's for, stupid." The teacher approached the children and entered the conversation first by listening and then by asking, "Can you go shopping in a store any time you feel like it?" Discussion led to the following conclusions: (1) you do not shop late at night because you have to sleep; and (2) stores have hours of shopping, to which people must pay attention (one tangential exchange on the last conclusion was "Except for robbers, they can go anytime," and the exasperated response, "But they're not *shopping,* they're stealing"). It was decided that the boy and girl plus two other children who had joined the discussion would take a walk around the block with the teacher in order to find the answer to her question, "How do you know when a store opens and when it closes?" They returned from their trip and as they entered the classroom, their newly gained information exploded: "It's on the door." "It's not the same for all the days." "They have a sign." Information was explored and shared. Signs posting store hours went up on several block buildings. One child posted times for visits to her house, fixing the hours around the baby's sleeping schedule. To end this anecdote, and also to indicate that an inner agenda is not given up so easily, when the girl came back to the fish store and asked, "What *are* your hours?" the response was, "I'm open one day a week, and today is not the open day."

2. Aside from other structures in the block scheme, there were a restaurant, a supermarket, and a farm. At the beginning of the week, when these structures were first built, no connections existed among them. In the daily discussion time that preceded work in the block area, the teacher asked the children operating the supermarket where their fruits, vegetables, and milk came from. Taking the question literally, they responded, "We draw all the things, and when we sell them all, we draw more." They were led to question where a real supermarket would get such items. "It comes on a truck." "The men put boxes on a long thing with wheels and the boxes go down to the cellar—whoosh!" "Vegetables come from the country because that's where the farmers are."

Following the discussion and the introduction of her questions, the teacher brought several books about farms into the classroom. Some children went on a trip to a small neighborhood grocery store. During the week, some of the children continued this investigation. One immediate response to the discussion occurred in the block scheme. The children operating the restaurant went to the supermarket to get their soda supply. It was several block schemes later before any store owner from the city went to a farm to buy supplies. Actually, the beginning connection was made in a most delightful way. A boy who was

working his farm became tired of waiting for other children to come and visit him, so he took his cow from door to door in the city and sold milk on the spot.

Teacher functioning is not sharply delineated; invariably there is overlapping of roles. For example, in the second illustration, the teacher was both a catalyst, in raising questions that were related to the children's activities, and a synthesizer, in that from her overall perspective of the block scheme, she could lead children to finding connections in their knowledge of reality and in their re-creation of it in dramatic play. The teacher wisely did not push her questioning past the children's interest or their ability to assimilate information. In this second anecdote, the children gathered most of their information vicariously through books and discussion rather than from direct experiences; therefore, they needed more time and opportunities for understanding. Buying soda from a store was within the realm of their experiences; their experiences were then stretched to include another set of relationships among consumers—a store buying from a store. To see a connection between farm, store, and restaurant was too abstract, and the children therefore could not act upon it.

In the first example, we saw the teacher as a guide leading the children toward resolution of their conflict—not by giving ready-made answers but by bringing to the children's awareness factors that might be considered and offering the opportunity for discovery through direct experience. It might have been simpler to have stated, "Stores have regular hours. Let's make a sign that will tell people when to come to your fish store." By so doing the teacher would have deprived the children not only of the possibility for research and discovery but also the opportunity to explore further the social aspects of the situation. Transferred to another material, it is the difference to be found between giving a child a jar of pink paint and offering an empty jar and some red and white paint.

In observing children's buildings and the interaction in their dramatic play, the teacher may see where children are and what they have done with the experiences they have had. The teacher is offered a truly personalized opportunity, flexible and open ended, in which to evaluate a child's learning. Within such an evaluation the teacher may consider and plan for the next steps to be taken to ensure continuity in the child's experiences and learning. Cognizant of the child's level of development and experiences, the teacher uses such planning to try to answer questions such as, Does this child need more *information* or more *time* in order to proceed? How frequently has this child built a house? Has it been the *same* each time? Should I intervene? If I do, shall it be directly or by introducing another child? Why is it that this child rarely builds a structure that can stand? At this moment, with this child, should I try to introduce more reality in the play? Or is this a time when I merely think about it and take no action, directly or indirectly? Why is it that when these two children build together, no matter what they start, it seems to end up as a

By asking a question related to the child's activities, the teacher may serve as a catalyst; yet the adult must take care not to push his questioning beyond the child's interest or ability to assimilate information.

91

jail? What kind of experience would be helpful to this small group trying to work out traffic patterns on the highway?

There are no ready answers or formulas. Each question must be answered individually in relation to a unique human being. What may be offered are a few general considerations, such as, How accurate is my observation? How well have I recorded, either mentally or in my notes? Is my question a reflection of something I am sensing rather than seeing? Can I pinpoint more accurately what I am feeling? What else does this child do during the day? Am I sufficiently aware of what this child's life is like outside school? How do I balance this child's needs with my considerations for the group? On what am I basing my expectations?

What is required of the teacher is that self-awareness and sensitivity toward others be exercised and refined and that minds be kept open not only to the activities of children but also to their vision and originality. What is offered to the teacher in the activities of block building and dramatic play is the opportunity to assist children in their search for clarity and understanding in a manner that is compatible to the learning style of the age and with activities that directly connect to those feelings and interests that are relevant and important to the child. Dewey, contrasting traditional and progressive education, presented certain principles that are appropriate to this topic:

> To imposition from above is opposed expression and cultivation of individuality; to external discipline is opposed free activity; to learning from texts and teachers, learning through experience; to acquisition of isolated skills and techniques by drill is opposed acquisition of them as means of attaining ends which make direct vital appeal; to preparation for a more or less remote future is opposed making the most of opportunities of present life; to static aims and materials is opposed acquaintance with a changing world. (Dewey [1938] 1963, 19–20)

Supporting the teacher's role

To what resources may teachers turn for assistance as they work with children in a block area? Questions, discussions, and the reactions of other children all help to stimulate play, but there are also many times when a teacher senses the need for something else to support or spark play.

As stated at the beginning of this chapter, for the young child there are few substitutes for direct experience. A young child will learn more from a real flower than from a picture of a flower. A picture may accurately record color, shape, and detail, but it cannot capture what the flower smells like, whether the petals feel smooth or furry, or how the flower may yield to the wind. Yet there are many times when a direct experience is not possible, so teachers must turn to other means to support children's learning. When books and pictures are used as sources, the teacher's job is to help the child *connect* information gathered vicariously with information gained from direct experience. Some books are chosen because of their explicit, factual nature; others because they evoke a mood and feelings. Similarly, a teacher may put up a detailed picture of a bridge clearly showing span, towers, and riverbanks, *and* a painting of a bridge partially hidden by patches of fog—with the illusion of twilight.

Still another opportunity for guiding and sparking interest in blocks exists through the use of props or supplementary materials in play. These materials add those touches of reality—the details—that help to give form to children's ideas. With the exception of the rubber or wooden people and animals, colored cubes and some transportation materials, batteries, and pulleys, most other supplementary materials may come from the children's woodwork, the use of Plasticine, paper and crayons, and all those things of which teachers are notorious collectors—plastic containers, cans, egg cartons, empty spools, pieces of cloth, wrapping paper, wool, and string. For example, I recall the inventiveness of a child who built a beauty parlor with five hair dryers under which sat five rubber people on small square blocks. The dryers were made of small plastic cups (collected from the weekly ice cream dessert) that had been taped onto pillar blocks.

Choosing the type of supplementary materials to be used raises the question of structured or unstructured materials. For example, in the block area, does the teacher buy the small dollhouse furniture—beds, tables, chairs, and television—or are children encouraged to create their own furniture with blocks or at the workbench? Does the teacher buy the sets of traffic signals available in catalogs, or do children make their own? The basic question is whether children are to be encouraged to use raw materials from which they may create their props or whether children are to be provided with ready-made props for use. In the unstructured, raw-material approach to materials, the child's imagination is used to change form and to create. The child has the opportunity to make a personal statement that may grow as the child's knowledge widens. Ready-made furniture is static in the sense that it remains at the level of the manufacturer's conception. With such materials, the child's imagination is used to put things together rather than in changing form and creating.

Teachers may have a common goal for the children in their classes—that they be able to create many of the supplementary items they use in block play from wood, string, paper, blocks, and other materials. What must be remembered in planning is that although teachers' goals create a framework for classroom functioning, the children of the class will differ in their ability to meet these goals. Some children will be able to meet the challenge immediately; some will follow the model set by other children and then act on their own initiative; others will need some teacher support and suggestions; and some children will not know how to function with raw materials. Many children, for a variety of reasons, have great difficulty making that imaginative leap—to make something out of something—and cannot proceed without a clearly defined, realistic base. In such instances, a teacher adhering to an unstructured approach may have to evaluate her or his goal with perspective. *Which is the ultimate goal—to have the child able to use blocks freely in building and dramatic play or to create props out of raw materials?* If focus stays on the latter goal, then the whole might be missed by concentrating on one part.

For some children, unstructured materials cause a dilemma rather than serve the purpose of stimulating play—not unlike the

Some teachers provide a variety of ready-made props—furniture, traffic signals, vehicles, and the like—for children to use in their block play; other teachers choose to provide only unstructured materials that children can use to fashion such items.

blocked writer facing a blank sheet in the typewriter. For each, an opening must be found from which ideas may flow. For some children, *their* ideas cannot begin unless they have a realistic model and the direct and continued guidance of the teacher. With such support, openings are made possible. Unstructured materials provide children with greater learning opportunities than do ready-made materials, but they also create difficulties for some children. The task is not to alter the goal or destination but to be aware that there are different ways of getting there.

> The teacher's business is to see that the occasion is taken advantage of. Since freedom resides in the operations of intelligent observation and judgment by which a purpose is developed, guidance given by the teacher to the exercise of the pupils' intelligence is an aid to freedom, not a restriction upon it. (Dewey [1938] 1963, 71)

Blocks and primary-grade children

Anecdotal illustrations of block play in this chapter have been drawn most frequently from classrooms of 4- to 6-year-olds, but blocks are not restricted to these ages. On the contrary, the activities begun in these early ages, the budding processes described, may reach a fullness in the primary grades, which are marvelously exciting. Structures that may exist for a couple of hours for 4-year-olds or a week for 5-year-olds may live on for a couple of weeks in the sustained, intricately planned activities of primary-grade children. With older children, research takes on greater depth, and reality in itself becomes a moving force. A living city may grow, complete with battery-operated streetlights, buzzing telephones, subway systems, and a municipal government.

In one such scheme in which a group of children re-created aspects of their life in New York City, the children brought the current events of the actual city—a milk strike—into the life of their block city. Information, ideas, and feelings about the milk strike were explored and clarified as the children re-created the strike situation in the block city and tried to find resolution for this conflict. Discussions and explanations grew out of their interaction with the issues as they participated in their re-created strike in a way that was not possible in the real milk strike. Of course, the children did not come to fully understand the complex political and economic factors involved in the strike, but they did reach a greater level of understanding than would have occurred had their involvement been solely on a verbal level. As Piaget has cautioned,

> This is a big danger of school—false accommodation which satisfies a child because it agrees with a verbal formula he has been given. This is a false equilibrium which satisfies a child by accommodating to words to authority and not to objects as they present themselves to him. . . . A teacher would do better not to correct a child's schemes, but to provide situations so he will correct them himself. (in Ripple & Rockcastle 1964, 4)

As children move on to the middle years of childhood and beyond, the need to imaginatively re-create experience and to externalize feelings and thoughts does not diminish. A changed perspective, increased skills, and a firmer grasp on reality contribute to altering the forms of expression. What was experienced in dramatic play may now be transferred to the original, child-created plays that may grow out of social studies. Thus the child may continue to fuse knowledge, feelings, and fantasy, breathing life and continuity into what is known. The child has come full circle to once again participating directly in play, but it is with an objectivity that was not possible earlier and from this vantage point the child experiences not only her or his knowledge but also the cumulative process of self-identity.

The changing landscape of play

In the more than 20 years since publication of the first edition of *The Block Book* in 1974, there has been considerable activity in the field of early education as we have reviewed, defined, and redefined curriculum for young children. In these two decades, the theorists influencing our work have shifted gradually; Vygotsky and Bruner now are quoted more frequently then Piaget. The sociocultural perspective influencing our current work complements the increased attention we give to the diversity of society and is evident in our efforts to make the education of young children multicultural, inclusive, and antibias.

95

We have become more articulate and assertive in our efforts to stop the downward push for academics and workbooks in kindergarten as activities and programs are evaluated in relation to NAEYC's guidelines for developmentally appropriate practices (Bredekamp 1987). And our daily teacher talk, among ourselves and with parents and administrators, now includes a vocabulary of *emergent literacy, themes, projects, writing process,* and *whole language.*

Interwoven in present discussions of these varied topics and approaches to teaching and learning, play continues to be a central point of interest. That children's play is included in discussions about curriculum for young children certainly is not a new idea. Play and learning have been connected throughout the history of early childhood education, from the mid-1800s to the present. What is different is how this cornerstone of the education of young children is now being viewed and utilized. It is not children's attitudes toward play or their joy in playing that have changed. Rather, I believe it is we, the adults, who have altered the landscape in which children play and, as a consequence, are subtly influencing the nature and function of children's play in our classrooms. In making this statement I am asking that, in the midst of all our activity and talk, we pause to think about play and review our expectations concerning young children, learning, and knowledge. Reflecting on practice is an essential part of teaching. Through our self-questioning, we clarify and make sense of our teaching and connect the *what* of teaching—the everyday reality and activities of our classrooms—with the *what for* of teaching—our knowledge, our values, and our aims (Bussis, Chittenden, & Amarel 1976).

Scripts for play

When the first part of this chapter was written in 1974, I included a description of one child's interactions within the reality created by children in a kindergarten block scheme. As described on p. 83 of this chapter, the children built homes, as well as a school, supermarket, fire department, playground, hospital, department of sanitation, and police station. The different buildings provided many opportunities for a variety of interactions and dramatic play among the children. The parenthetical remarks, included in the itemizing of this imagined world the children had created, described how one child encountered and interacted with the various buildings and services. In these encounters and interactions within dramatic play the scripts for play grew out of the children's interests, questions, experiences, and thoughts and feelings about the social and physical world. In the social reality they created, their play became a means for making sense of the world and their place in it.

An observer of these children's dramatic play in the block area over the course of a week might have described it as "child-centered play." This often-used phrase ignores the role of the teacher. Although less visible, the dynamic contributions of the teacher also were present in the children's play. She created the stage, the setting for play, by providing ample time, space, and materials; planned the daily discussions that became a forum for raising questions, solving problems, and stretching thinking; and arranged small- and whole-group trips to expand the children's perspective through direct experiences. Through her continued observations, assessments, reflection, and knowledge of development and of skills and content, the teacher supported, guided, and extended the children's play. What existed over the course of the week, and in the time before and after this particular block scheme, was a *partnership*, a transactional relationship between children and teacher in the development of curriculum over time—time for both to experience, think, plan, experiment, and try out possibilities.

Themes and projects

Children are still building and playing. The question that surfaces from observations in classrooms and from reading the current literature on curriculum is: Whose script is being played? More and more frequently, the script for dramatic play grows out of teachers' brainstorming, curriculum webs, planned themes and projects, or children's interests.

My visits to a classroom of 6-year-olds over a period of several weeks provide an example of the interweaving of themes or projects within the curriculum. *Post office* was the theme chosen by the teacher, based on the interests of several children. The children took trips to the post office and then engaged in a variety of activities using the information they had gathered. They made drawings, paintings, and a mural about the post office. With cardboard and hollow blocks they constructed a post office that they could enter, participating directly in dramatic play. There was much talk, writing, and storytelling about the post office. In the block area, a group of children built a large post office that included a great deal of accurate detail. Using the scaled wooden people, the children set up "postal workers" who offered various services to "customers" mailing packages and letters. In both the block play and the other activities, the children actively participated and used the information they had gained.

Here I would like to contrast dramatic play and block building as it occurs when children build a post office as *one structure within a setting* that contains other buildings and services, with a post office that is the *only structure in the block area*. In the block scheme and the dramatic play interactions described in the earlier edition of this chapter, a variety of structures were located in the block area. Each child's building represented some aspect of community living—homes, services, and stores. Questions surfaced in the interactions among the children in the social reality they created. When is the supermarket open? Where do I put my garbage, and then what happens to it? What does the doctor do in the hospital? How does the mail get to the post office? How does the mail carrier know where to deliver the mail? Questions and problems multiply in a diverse social setting.

In contrast, when a post office is built as the only structure in the block area, it exists *out of context*. There are no other structures to elicit interactions and questions. Building a solitary structure in the block area eliminates the complex and unexpected possibilities, the questions and problems, that arise and grow out of the social interactions of dramatic play. When there are no other buildings, to whom are the letters and packages mailed? With no other structures (and no "people") present, what would give rise to the need to communicate with others? And there would be no impetus to deal with logistical problems, such as schedules for pickup and delivery and the need for and placement of mailboxes. The decontextualized, solitary post office is a *model* rather than a living structure.

The question remains: Whose script guides or directs dramatic play? Implicit in this question are others. Where are the openings in the curriculum for children to ask *their* questions, questions that grow out of their concerns, their dilemmas, their curiosity, their views of the world? Where is the partnership between children and teacher? And, one may ask, is it possible that, in a group of 25 six-year-olds, all the children are interested in the post office?

A view from another culture

Since 1991 I have been involved in a research project in Iceland with early childhood teachers and my colleague Jónina Tryggvadóttir, a member of the faculty of the College for Preschool Teachers in Reykjavik (Fósturskoli Islands). My experience in another culture has made the changes in children's play that I have described even more striking.

Until 1991, unit building blocks were generally not used in Icelandic playschools (in Iceland all early childhood settings for children under age 6 are called "playschools"). If blocks were available they were similar in shape and size to American small table blocks. Following a one-week course I taught in block building and dramatic play, in which 25 early childhood teachers and 5 faculty from the College for Preschool Teachers built with blocks and discussed children's play and their educational aims, two playschools received unit blocks. This "new" material was added to the playschools' existing activities and materials, which consisted of a great variety of art materials; a traditional "house" area for dramatic play with props for dressup; many manipulatives; books; cooking materials; a spacious room for large-muscle activities which also served as a room where several groups could come together for singing and other events; and a well-equipped outdoor area.

The teachers in the two schools were asked to keep journals to record their thoughts, questions, and reactions as the blocks were introduced into the curriculum. The teachers also wrote logs describing the children's work with blocks. Logs and journals were written over a six-month period. In addition, about every six weeks, Jónina met with the five teachers in the project and a representative of the Early Childhood Council of Reykjavik (Dagvist Barna). In the group meetings, the teachers from the two playschools shared their questions, problems, reactions, and anecdotal material.

Although the style of the Icelandic children's buildings, the architecture of their structures, differed in some pronounced ways from American children's buildings (speaking in general terms), commonality between cultures was evident in what children chose to represent symbolically. The children in Iceland built homes, restaurants, and stores. Reflecting their own particular environment and culture, the children also built the churches, swimming pools, and outdoor camping sites found throughout their country. Their play also included elements from the culture of television and movies—superheroes and cartoon figures. The developmental stages with which we are familiar were evident from

Great richness and complexity emerge in children's play when the children themselves create the context and scripts for their dramas within the permeable structure and setting offered by the teachers.

the child about to be 2, who simply walked around holding a block, to the older 5-year-olds, who built elaborate, detailed farms and shopping malls.

Observing the children's interactions and listening to their conversations, the teachers were amazed to discover how much knowledge the children possessed, the depth of their thinking and questioning, and the range of their curiosity and interests. As the children created their social world in the block area through the structures they built, as they interacted with each other in dramatic play, they presented and represented their view and understanding of the social and physical world in which they lived. In their dramatic play the children brought to the

surface their personal themes and questions, their thoughts and feelings, in a manner the teachers had not seen before. The following anecdote of a group of 5-year-olds is an example of the kind of discussions and complex thinking that occurred in the children's play and surprised the teachers.

It was the week before Easter and Karl built a church (with a nearby small swimming pool). He invited children from the other buildings to come to his church service. Taking their wooden people and placing them in the pews, they joined Karl, the minister, for the service and together they sang hymns. Karl talked to the parishioners about God and then asked God to bless his church. After the blessing, Karl and Gunnar began to argue about who had sung better.

Róbert: There is just one way to find out. First Karl will sing. Then Gunnar will sing.

(Gunnar and Karl follow Róbert's suggestion.)

Inga: Now we had a singing contest in the church, and I don't think God will like it in His church.

Karl: It is my church and I will decide if there is a singing contest in my church.

Helga: Karl, you built the church, but if you build a church, you build it for God.

Róbert: I don't think that God would mind if there is a singing contest in the church.

A heated discussion among the five children followed, too rapid for the teacher to record each child's comment. Finally, they solved the dilemma. The children decided that it would be permissible to have a contest in a church but only if they sang hymns.

The teachers' logs contained many examples of children making meaningful connections and of their knowledge and thinking about current events in the city, Icelandic history, nature, and imagined "experiment(s) with the world to find out what it is like" (Dewey [1916] 1966, 140). Such richness and complexity surfaced in the children's play because the context and the scripts for the various dramas were created by the children within the permeable structure and setting offered by the teachers. It is not surprising that in final interviews and in their group meetings, the teachers spoke often of how block building and the social interactions of dramatic play offered many opportunities to support the realization of their aims in the area of moral development.

Research on play

In recent years there has been an increase in the number of books on play (Monighan-Nourot, Scales, Van Hoorn, & Almy 1987; Kelly-Byrne 1989; Klugman & Smilansky 1990; Scales, Almy, Nicolopoulou, & Ervin-Tripp 1991; Jones & Reynolds 1992). As play is studied in greater depth and detail and from different perspectives, the connections between play and learning in various academic areas and in the acquisition of many skills have been strengthened and made more explicit. I wonder whether this detailing and explication have contributed to changing the landscape of play and our view of its purpose.

With our informed awareness of the rich potential and power of play for learning, we seem to be using play for specific learnings and, in the process, shifting the balance between teaching and learning. What I observe and read about the activities growing out of themes and projects is the use of a play *modality* rather than play itself. Though children are active participants, their play is governed in large measure by a delivered theme carefully thought through and planned by adults. It seems to me that in many instances what we have is the *appearance* of play rather than its essence. Children are active. Gone are the dittos and workbooks. Materials are present in abundance, as are the opportunities for the use of varied skills. There are many choices—in what to do, which material to use, what story to write, what aspect to dramatize. But children's choices are bound by the parameters of the chosen and delivered theme or project. Their questions, their experiences, their meaning-making must connect to the given.

A further issue arises in relation to knowledge: the choice of content. From observations, talks with colleagues, and discussions with students in the courses I teach, the themes and projects that appear in early childhood classrooms are quite diverse and eclectic. I have seen, heard, or read about themes and projects involving dinosaurs, bears, potatoes, post offices, vegetables, popcorn, hospitals, the beach, and fairy tales. Some projects or themes take place over one week, others extend over longer periods of time. In this abundance of diverse topics it is difficult at times to discern some connection between chosen topics or themes, some sense of continuity, some framework into which these various topics may be interwoven. Possibly the framework I seek is the wholeness and continuity implicit in *social studies*, with its focus on the human world, on people's work and lives situated in the context of culture and society. Learning about the human world with all its complexities offers children the opportunity to deal with concepts such as *community, equity, interdependence,* and *responsibility*—ideas and values essential to a democratic society.

My concerns about knowledge, the content we choose for our curriculum and how it is constructed, are echoed in the work of Edelsky, Altwerger, and Flores (1991). In their perceptive analysis of the theory and practices connected to whole language, they make an astute distinction between theme *units* and theme *cycles.* "In thematic units, the topics are used for teaching subjects or skills" (p. 64). In their example of a unit on bears, bears provide the "glue" that connects science, reading, math, literature, and other areas. Units tend to be "skills-driven," full of activities related to the topic. With theme cycles, "it is just the reverse: subjects and skills (science, math, reading, etc.) are used for investigating the topic" (pp. 64–65). Cycles develop out of curiosities and fundamental, probing questions, such as those that grow out of social studies. In highlighting the distinction between units and cycles, the authors note,

> We add census data to learn about the populations; we do not find out about population totals in order to have a reason to add numbers together. (Edelsky, Altwerger, & Flores 1991, 65)

As I think about our work with children and about knowledge and the honoring of children's play, questions—and choices—surface. Is play to be used as a means for the learning of essential skills and the delivering of chosen content? Is it in children's play—their play—that we seek to find opportunities for the development of skills and the construction of knowledge? How do we define and balance the partnership between children and teachers in the development of curriculum so that voices, personal meanings, and interests on either side are not lost? What knowledge about the world do we welcome in our classrooms?

The learning opportunities available in block building and dramatic play are rich and varied. My purpose in raising these questions is not to create more either/ors with which we must contend. Rather it is to acknowledge that teaching is filled with decisionmaking and that the choices we make, the opportunities we offer, have consequences for the kinds of experiences the children shall have in our classrooms.

References

Bredekamp, S. 1987. *Developmentally appropriate practice in early childhood programs serving children from birth through age 8.* Washington, DC: NAEYC.

Bruner, J.S. 1986. *Actual minds, possible worlds.* Cambridge, MA: Harvard University Press.

Bussis, A.M., E.A. Chittenden, & M. Amarel. 1976. *Beyond surface curriculum.* Boulder, CO: Westview.

Dewey, J. [1938] 1963. *Experience and education.* London: Collier-Macmillan.

Dewey, J. [1916] 1966. *Democracy and education.* New York: Macmillan, Free Press.

Edelsky, C., B. Altwerger, & B. Flores. 1991. *Whole language: What's the difference?* Portsmouth, NH: Heinemann.

Isaacs, S. 1966. *Intellectual growth in young children.* New York: Schocken.

Isaacs, S. 1972. *Social development in young children.* New York: Schocken.

Johnson, H.M. [1933] 1966. *The art of block building.* New York: Bank Street College of Education (chapter 2, this volume).

Jones, E., & G. Reynolds. 1992. *The play's the thing: Teachers' roles in children's play.* New York: Teachers College Press.

Kelly-Byrne, D. 1989. *A child's play life: An ethnographic study.* New York: Teachers College Press.

Klugman, E., & E. Smilansky, eds. 1990. *Children's play and learning: Perspectives and policy implications.* New York: Teachers College Press.

Lowenfeld, M. 1967. *Play in childhood.* New York: Wiley.

Monighan-Nourot, P., B. Scales, J. Van Hoorn, & M. Almy. 1987. *Looking at children's play: A bridge between theory and practice.* New York: Teachers College Press.

Pratt, C. 1948. *I learn from children.* New York: Simon & Schuster.

Ripple, R.E., & V.N. Rockcastle, eds. 1964. *Piaget rediscovered.* Conference on Cognitive Studies and Curriculum Development, Cornell University and the University of California.

Scales, B., M. Almy, A. Nicolopoulou, & S. Ervin-Tripp. 1991. *Play and the social context of development in early care and education.* New York: Teachers College Press.

Vygotsky, L.S. [1933] 1966. Play and its role in the mental development of the child. *Soviet Psychology* 12 (6): 62–76.

Vygotsky, L.S. [1934] 1986. *Thought and language,* trans. A. Kozulin. Cambridge, MA: MIT Press.

For further reading

Biber, B. 1967. A learning-teaching paradigm integrating intellectual and affective processes. In *Behavioral science frontiers in education,* eds. E.M. Bower & W.G. Hollister. New York: Wiley.

Biber, B. 1984. *Early education and psychological development.* New Haven, CN: Yale University Press.

Bruner, J.S., R. Olver, & P. Greenfield. 1966. *Studies in cognitive growth.* New York: Wiley.

Cuffaro, H.K. 1991. A view of materials as the texts of early childhood curriculum. In *Issues in early childhood curriculum,* eds. B. Spodek & O.N. Saracho, 64-85. New York: Teachers College Press.

Cuffaro, H.K. 1995. *Experimenting with the world: John Dewey and the early childhood classroom.* New York: Teachers College Press.

Edwards, C., L. Gandini, & G. Forman, eds. 1993. *The hundred languages of children: The Reggio Emilia approach to early childhood education.* Norwood, NJ: Ablex.

Griffiths, R. 1935. *Imagination in early childhood.* London: Routledge & Kegan Paul.

Herron, R.E., & B. Sutton-Smith. 1971. *Child's play.* New York: Wiley.

Isaacs, S. 1948. The nature and function of phantasy. *International Journal of Psychoanalysis 29 (part 2):* 73–96.

Katz, L.G., & S. Chard. 1989. *Engaging children's minds: The project approach.* Norwood, NJ: Ablex.

Millar, S. 1969. *The psychology of play.* London: Pelican.

Paris, C.L. 1993. *Teacher agency and curriculum making in classrooms.* New York: Teachers College Press.

Piaget, J. 1962. *Play, dreams and imitation in childhood.* New York: W.W. Norton.

Seefeldt, C. 1984. *Social studies for the preschool-primary child.* 2d ed. Columbus, OH: Merrill.

Shapiro, E., & B. Biber. 1972. The education of young children: A developmental-interaction approach. *Teachers College Record* 74 (1): 55–79.

Sutton-Smith, B. 1971. The playful modes of knowing. In *Play: The child strives toward self-realization,* ed. G. Engstrom, 13–25. Washington, DC: NAEYC.

7

Blocks in the Elementary School

Elizabeth Dreier

Although viewpoints in education may sometimes seem to swing with the pendulum of fashion, the most recent developments in the theory and research of human knowledge extend and deepen, but do not refute, the principal ideas of the philosophers who shaped modern education. That children need to be active and interactive learners—an idea expressed in the Deweyan phrase *learn by doing*—is confirmed in the burgeoning knowledge emerging from research based on Piagetian theory and on that grand compendium of disciplines known as *human information processing* (Bobrow & Collins 1975).

How children in the early elementary grades learn

Early elementary school-age children are concrete operational thinkers who learn to understand the world by actively engaging with that world. They manipulate, investigate, explore, test, and change. They want to see what will happen if . . . . Through this interaction children take in the information from which they build an inner model of the world; they also build the intellectual structures that will enable them to take in and integrate more sophisticated information.

Piagetian insights into the intellectual development of children have led educators to wonder how much development can be fostered. Researchers have found little success in direct training methods, but there is a solid body of evidence that indicates that social interaction among children working together to solve problems can help all of them move to higher levels of intellectual functioning.

As a result of extensive investigation of the effects of social interaction on cognitive development, Bearison concludes that "Knowledge is not constructed independently of the social contexts in which it is shared, confirmed, and used to mediate social discourse" (1982, 217) His subjects, children working on problems in spatial perspective, were more successful when they worked in pairs and groups than when they worked alone. The differences in children's points of view raised questions in their minds and caused them to articulate and clarify their own views in the course of justifying them, as well as to consider the views of others, which were often hotly defended. Sometimes the conflict resulted in completely new solutions not previously considered by either child.

Through the combined talents and efforts of psychologists and students of artificial intelligence and linguistics, we have learned that human memory is constructive rather than replicative (Bransford, Barclay, & Franks 1972; Bransford & McCarrell 1974). What we learn and recall to build on for further learning is the meaning we have made of our experiences rather than a photocopy of those experiences. People remember ideas, words, even images that they have never seen, if these ideas and images represent the sense they have made of an experience—what they believe it meant.

It is not surprising then that *how* we represent in our memory what we have learned is a very important part of the learning process. Cognitive psychologists use the term *schema* to describe how we organize our world knowledge in memory (Rumelhart & Ortory 1977). A schema is a plan, a script, a scenario, perhaps a kind of play. It is not linear or simple but complex and dynamic. Modern urban dwellers certainly have a schema for a restaurant. At it broadest level, a restaurant schema prescribes food being served, a surface to put it on, a place to sit, and, perhaps, utensils. In reading this description most readers will conjure up an image, rather vague, containing tables, chairs, and waiters moving about, as well as some seated diners. Being told that it is a Japanese restaurant or a luncheonette or a McDonald's will activate different, more specific, more detailed schemata. The reader will not have to be told that there are no tablecloths at McDonald's or that there are tablecloths at an expensive restaurant. How are these schemata built, enriched, extended, and refined? The question is important because it is exactly this extension and deepening that constitutes learning.

Children in the elementary-school years build these internal intellectual structures when they have rich opportunities to represent their ideas and new concepts in direct, concrete, physical ways and when they have opportunities to manipulate, alter, and interact with the ideas through their representations.

Science and mathematics programs in the modern school often reflect these insights of Piagetian and cognitive theory in the provision of concrete materials and firsthand experiences as essential tools for learning. How can we provide children with the opportunity for concrete interactions, for manipulation and investigation, if the subject is, for example, social studies? Concepts are abstract, distances are great, time frames are large, and events are often long past. This chapter will illustrate how blocks have singular potential for meeting this and other needs in elementary education.

Blocks in action

A class of urban second-graders, having explored their immediate environment in kindergarten and first grade, were ready for a more systematic investigation that would enable them to organize their immediate experiences into the more abstract concepts of a city and a more generalized understanding of the interrelationship of human functions within that city. Their block work was structured by the teacher. A rule was established that Block City would be real. Buildings must be of a kind that would be found in a city. Each child builder must find or make a toy person to represent her- or himself in the daily playing out of city life. Each daily session of block work was preceded by a class discussion, held in the meeting area, during which plans were made and many lively exchanges took place about what really happens in a city.

Children made accessories for their buildings, fleshing out their ideas from the basic materials supplied in neatly labeled boxes in the block area. Fruits and vegetables, all kinds of clothing, typewriters, stethoscopes, microcomputers, fire hoses, pooper-scoopers— the list of needs that emerged during the semester's work was, indeed, long and varied. The materials used were many and the methods inventive as children made these objects from paper, wood, clay, fabric, and many found materials. They worked in shop and studio as well as in their classroom.

After a day or two of work, building time was declared over, and all of the citizens of Block City engaged in the life and work that made their city go. On some days the interests and curiosity of the children were sufficient to ensure lively interchange. At other times, when energy seemed to be low or activities began to be repetitious, the teacher provided structure. There might be an assignment for the day: visit two recreation areas in the city, or buy two things today.

As these young children took part in the concrete representation of a process, questions arose that would not have occurred to them if their consideration of a topic had been only abstract. If all of the people have to buy something in Block City, where will they get the money? A shopkeeper's source of income quickly becomes evident, but how does the police officer get money? A second-grade group working on this problem had many vigorous discussions, speculated on possible solutions, investigated through the library and through firsthand interviews, and was introduced in a meaningful way to concepts of city services, taxes, and interdependence in a society.

Another group—fighting one of the Block City fires that engaged the imagination of children moving out of the protection of early childhood and concerned about the safety of venturing away from Mommy—wondered how the water got into the hydrant that so readily supplied their hoses. The study that emerged from this question was extensive. It took children to the street to find and count hydrants and utility covers; to the reservoir to see the pumping station and interview the workers there; and to the library to locate books, to read and be read to about the fascinating world under the city. They represented in their Block City at least a dozen different kinds of pipes, cables, and conduits that carry the water, steam, electricity, telephone lines, and other lifelines of the city, giving reality and substance to the magic of light switches and faucets. This investigation led to many other classroom explorations with water, focusing on sinking and floating, on evaporation and drying. The city is a complex environment, too easily seen by children as magical. Processes, sequences, and cause and effect are difficult to observe. Block City makes reality accessible.

The flexibility and appropriateness of blocks for supporting learning at many ages is readily seen in their use by 9- and 10-year-olds in another school, where the curriculum included a much more sophisticated study of New York City. In learning about their city's history, the fourth- and fifth-graders modeled early New York City, using many materials suited to the gabled buildings and cobblestone streets. When they began to study modern New York, they returned to the familiar unit blocks, which seemed singularly suited to represent the bricks, concrete, and steel of angular contemporary architecture. They wanted to build Lower Manhattan to compare dramatically and in detail with their model of New Amsterdam. They also wanted to show the important features of "uptown" and, finally, of other boroughs.

Using blocks to give physical form to their developing ideas enables elementary children to tackle complex problems, manipulate ideas, and integrate sophisticated concepts in mathematics and social studies.

Much thinking went into solving the problem of representing such a quantity of information in the limited space of the classroom while leaving some room for desks, chairs, and other more mundane but essential furniture. What a solid grasp of symbolization and the abstractions of mapping resulted from this exercise that engaged the imagination and reasoning powers of the whole class! The children decided on a combination of realistic and symbolic representation—a solution appropriate to their transitional intellectual stage and so important in helping them make this intellectual step in a real rather than a superficial and superimposed way.

In their three-dimensional model, Lower Manhattan was realistically represented, with detailed buildings complete with street addresses marked on the doors. Space and time limited this kind of representation, so they mapped the rest of the city, indicating major waterways, streets, and avenues, and representing with blocks the buildings and bridges they selected as important. Lively, often heated discussion centered on establishing criteria for importance. Gradually the children moved from "my house" to "our school" to consider the services, supplies, activities, and functions essential to urban life.

"You have to have stores, silly, or there would be nothing to eat!"

"Well, but what about hospitals?"

"And movie theaters!"

Like city councils, the children debated the role of the arts in human life.

"Is the opera house important enough to include?"

"What about gas stations?"

"They're not important."

"Oh, yeah, how can the cars go?"

The children encountered the complexities of economic interdependence.

Little by little the discussion turned to law and government. What really does go on in City Hall? They needed to know so that they could decide whether and how to include it in their city.

The final depiction involved symbols, a key, a scale, and a carefully worded indicator that the scale was different for the two parts of the model. This is a good example of the interaction between thought and action, between school-age children's growing capacity to deal with abstractions and their continuing need to ground such abstractions in concrete experience.

Far from holding these children back, the use of blocks to give physical form to their developing ideas enabled the children to tackle complex problems, manipulate ideas, and integrate sophisticated concepts in mathematics and social studies.

Third-graders became very interested in the river that ran next to their town. In their block area the children depicted the river, using carefully cut blue paper to follow its winding path. After many walking trips to the local piers, the children had the information they wanted about the neighboring town that was visible across the water and about the bridges that crossed their river. Their work led to many questions. Their dramatization of life in their Block Town awakened many interests. They built the warehouses and markets found along the wharves and furnished them with much produce and goods. They made boats, with careful attention to detail. Their interest in and growing knowledge about the many kinds of boats they saw on their trips led to increasingly elaborate woodworking. The children did not just make boats; they turned to books in the library for further details so that their models would have the authenticity that 8-year-olds want. This work led to much curiosity about where the cargo came from and eventually to the making of a large map of the United States, with symbols indicating the source of manufactured goods, food products, and raw materials that were brought to their community from around the country. This was a lesson in geography that had meaning and would be long remembered.

The same children wondered about the suspension bridge that spanned the river. While building it during block time, they noticed and speculated about the role of the suspension wires. Were they for decoration? What could they hold up if they were attached to the bridge? And perhaps even more important, where could the answers to their questions be found?

The teacher added this question to the growing list kept on a large chart in the classroom. The group speculated about sources of information. One child went off to the library to look under *B* in the card catalog.

"Try *S* for suspension," a classmate called out to him.

"Let's ask the man who owns the bridge" was another suggestion.

They learned about city government, about its departments and jurisdictions and sources of funding. As citizens, they had first experiences in using their municipal services to obtain information and received a wonderful letter from the local bridge authority. Turning to more immediate sources for further information, the group visited the high school physics teacher's classroom and subsequently received a visit from a classmate's engineer father as their guest. With what concentration and purpose they took notes—a first experience with this research skill! Finally they built a suspension bridge and tested its load-bearing capacities with Matchbox cars. Were these lessons in civics? physics? language arts? Who is to say where such vital learning begins and ends?

Relationship of block building to the curriculum

The benefits of block building are not confined to any single academic discipline. The full range of middle-grade studies can be enriched and extended by the thoughtful inclusion of blocks as a curriculum tool.

Research and writing. The basic research skills of locating, organizing, and reporting information are difficult for many children. Teachers struggle to convey to children the complex skill of note taking. How do they know what to write down? Teachers struggle, too, to help children know what is meant by *putting it in your own words*. Many elementary-age children find it hard to know how to decide what information is important, so they copy text onto note cards because young researchers have no purpose of their own to guide their choice. We naturally put ideas into

In the course of planning or building a city or other complex construction, children often encounter questions or problems that require further research.

our own words when we have integrated the information. And human learners integrate what makes sense. So, to learn research skills, children must be engaged in a real quest.

Perhaps the biggest struggle centers on helping children learn to organize ideas in a report. This very abstract ability eludes and confuses many children. Two qualities make abstract experience accessible to school-age children: purpose and a concrete referent. Representation of important new learnings in block building meets both of these criteria. Children seek information in response to their own very immediate and concrete ques-

tions. In the beginning these questions arise spontaneously during block play, and the teacher is a major guide in the search for answers. Quite quickly, children become able to use book pictures, simple print, and the card catalog on their own. Because the children formulate the questions, they have little trouble knowing what is important. Because they want to hold on to the new idea, to report to their group, or to solve their own problem in blocks, they quickly learn to make a note or two. Because the notes serve their purposes, there is not so much confusion about what words to use or what bit of information is worth recording. In such meaningful early experiences, children build a set of expectations about what research is all about. They do not see it as a school chore, in which the goal is to fill the number of note cards required by the teacher, according to some mysterious criterion. They establish a solid conviction that research is the meaningful quest for information for real purposes. Such children will soon begin to establish some organizational principles of their own and will see real sense in the formal skills lessons that are also necessary.

Research in reading comprehension supports the view that the reader's previous knowledge and understandings influence the reading process (Kintsch & Van Dijk 1978). World knowledge, organized into schema, is essential to the reading process. Schemata— or internal representations of events, objects, and ideas—are built and elaborated on by children who have acquired concrete operations through real-world experiences. Complexity of association and vividness of experience determine the accessibility and sophistication of the schema.

Children in the middle grades begin to encounter abstract ideas in their content-area reading. Concepts of government, economics, trade and barter, time and distance, properties of materials, and the functions of structures are all increasingly evident in the tests children in these grades are given. All of these concepts are exemplified in the block activities described here. The opportunities to develop clear, personally meaningful, and elaborated concepts—or schemata—to support the understanding of real abstractions is limited only by the range and depth of topics studied. It is almost a cliché in education that children read and understand what is close to their own experience. Blocks are a way of bringing complex ideas about the distant and long-ago world into the experience of children.

Opportunities for writing abound in the busy life of block cities. There are bookstores, libraries, publishing houses, and newspapers. One group of 9-year-olds produced sets of carefully written miniature storybooks. Another class published a block-city newspaper and decided that it should be the size of a real newspaper. Events of the city were described, merchandise was advertised, and municipal problems were discussed in editorials. The class studied real dailies to learn about format and to see what kind of articles they may want to write. They stretched to cope with the reading level of their local paper, but it was worth it for such an interesting enterprise. Of course, their own newspaper required careful editing and proofreading, and the children rotated these chores, so every child had plenty of this valuable experience. Proofreading was done with a much better eagle eye than is commonly brought to such a chore in an early childhood setting. There were even arguments about the finer points of punctuation!

Scientific principles. Many practical problems in the building and use of a block city can be solved by the application of scientific principles. Buildings can be wired for electricity, and streets can be lit by a connected series of streetlamps. The group that provided these utilities for their block city used library skills, reading for content, and much direct experimentation with bulbs, wires, and batteries before they were satisfied with the quality and reliability of their service. Children devised and used ramps, pulleys, and levers, activities that provide real understanding of the workings and purposes of simple machines and a good beginning grasp of mechanics. Science in action of this kind is frequently seen in its early forms in kindergarten block building. Older children, carrying their investigations much further, need systematic variation in their trials and rigor in recording their findings. Their discoveries are more sophisticated and involve the elaboration of concepts that build a solid foundation for classification, prediction, and hypothesis testing, which are essential to later work in science and to all clear thinking. In one school, 5-year-olds were delighted to lift their elevator by pulling its string by hand through a simple pulley. Fourth-graders wanted theirs to be raised by an erector-set motor that a classmate had brought in. The blocks were heavy for the limited power of the small motor, so the children learned to rig a double pulley and at the same time learned a real appreciation of the relationship between distance, time, and work that underlies the usefulness of simple machines. How much more meaning the formulas that symbolize these relationships will have when they are encountered in high-school physics! And how much less mysterious they will be!

Mathematical skills and concepts. Concepts of size and scale are worked through and developed in block-building activities of all kinds. Beginning block builders deal in broad approximations and consider notions of comparative size as they represent daily life in their structures. House furnishings and details such as doors have to fit the people who live in the houses. Cars and garages must have at least a rough proportion. These ideas are gradually refined through many experiences, much discussion, and some argument. Children in the upper elementary grades who have had such experiences are ready to deal with problems of size, scale, ratio, and proportion with precision and system. Grids that grow out of representations of city streets, often taped on the primary classroom floor, set the stage for solid mastery of mapping and graphing, as coordinates are developed and used by young city planners. The block city, the concrete referent, allows the move to abstraction to take place with confidence and flexibility of application. Children who have developed and used coordinates in response to real problems integrate abstract understanding of this and other tools and have them available in their repertoire of problem-solving techniques rather than seeing them as the limited interests of the algebra teacher.

Buying and selling—and later, banking—provide many practical applications of computational skills. A fifth-grade class moved into the study of percents earlier than their curriculum plan provided because they needed to compute interest in connection with their banking activity in Block City. Another group, somewhat younger, worked out a beginning understanding of percentage in order to hold sales in their shops.

Measurement is extensive and varied. Area, perimeter, height, weight, time, and distance are considered in real situations. Children gradually move from arbitrary units to precise use of standard measures. A common rule in early block building prohibits buildings taller than a child. Ingenious builders soon ask, "Which child?" and encounter the need for standard units. Older children devise increasingly rigorous building codes in response to the pressures of scarce space and the limits of building materials. They use rulers, yardsticks, meter sticks, and tapes, and learn not only to use and read these tools but also to choose the most efficient one for each task. Making lakes and swimming pools is one example of activities that have stimulated children's thoughtful consideration of problems of volume and capacity. A team charged

In creating a block building or city, children encounter many practical problems that call for application of scientific principles; for instance, they devise ramps, pulleys, and levers, and even wire their buildings for electricity.

with providing their town with a water tower realized that they had to consider the weight their tower would bear, and they devised ingenious methods for weighing water as well as computing the capacity of their container.

The role of the teacher

Because block building is so often thought of as a free-choice activity for young children, teachers wonder what role they can and should play in a classroom block period for older children. The more experience the children have had with blocks, the more they benefit from structure and direction. Some of the areas in which structure for block use can be provided are described here.

Planning and discussion periods. All or most sessions of block use should begin and/or end with a group discussion. Topics can include planning for building; resolution of problems that have arisen during an activity period; assignments for the day; distribution of goods, services, labor, and materials; ways to find needed information; additional details or accessories needed; ways to extend the block city to incorporate the children's growing body of knowledge; record keeping; and many more.

Kinds of buildings. Young children can profit from sorting out reality from fantasy when they are asked to build only what can be found in a real city.

Older children can take part in decisions about what can and should be included. Is their city contemporary or representative of an earlier time? Are buildings to be authentic? Shall there be more than one of the same kind? Are there limits on height? size?

Topical focus. First- and second-graders, thinking in terms of how human needs are met in a city, may think with their teacher about buildings that are needed. Later the teacher may choose a focus, for example, "This week all our buildings need to show how food is available in the city." Schools, hospitals, fire stations, and office buildings can demonstrate food sources. This project can spark thought, research, discussion, production of many detailed accessories, and many questions for further study. In addition, it can produce interaction among citizens of the city as, for example, the hospital staff plans how they will stock and staff their kitchen. For older elementary children, the topical focus can be chosen in group discussion, can be broader, and can serve over a longer period. "How are raw materials brought to our city?" In a class of 9- and 10-year-olds, each citizen can refer to this question, apply it to her or his own enterprise, do research to fill information gaps, and plan with other children to represent jointly the kind of transportation that will meet their common need to bring materials from a distance.

Number of children. The teacher has an important role in establishing guidelines about how many children can be involved in a project. In some classrooms all children build and then live in a block city together. Much interesting interaction takes place, and the activity is given significance as a real tool for learning. In other classrooms the teacher sees more benefit in the use of the area by teams or small groups, who then share with their classmates in a meeting. There may be one project seen to completion by a team, which is followed by another team, tackling another problem. Or children may work in relays on specific, assigned parts of an overall group project. Here is an opportunity for the teacher to see that all children gain experience with the extensive possibilities in the block area.

Rules for block city living. This is an area of great potential for children's moral development. Problems arise in block cities, as in any community. Space is scarce and must be shared. Commodities are not unlimited. "I need more doubles!" says one architect, who finds they have all been used. Another wants the very truck that a neighbor has found in the neatly labeled boxes stored on a shelf near the block area. Traffic poses as much difficulty to young citizens as to big-city mayors! All of these problems are topics for group discussion. One class of 7-year-olds invented streets and zoning laws to control the chronic knocking down of buildings caused by congestion in their city. A grid was carefully laid out on the floor with masking tape, and the group decided on a rule limiting the number and size of buildings per lot. Ten-year-olds can generalize and categorize issues and document solutions—for example, make rules about space or sharing materials and amend and revise them.

Sometimes the solutions that children develop do not coincide with adult judgments.

A third-grade class had frequent arguments about the assignment of roles in their block city. Too many children wanted to be mayor; not enough elected to clean the streets. Together the children decided to allocate jobs by lottery and to allow for no changes, ever. Although the teacher anticipated that dissatisfaction would soon arise about the permanent nature of role assignments, he decided to let the children encounter this problem on their own. Very soon the class found that yet another meeting was necessary. They developed a rotation system, allowing everyone to try out all the jobs that their lively city required.

The teacher must be sensitive in deciding when to protect the children from consequences that may be too much for them to handle and when to let them live with and evaluate their own rules—and learn by doing so. Children who are active in developing rules have an appropriate understanding and respect for the meaning of laws. They see that laws are devised by human ingenuity in response to human problems. They recognize that laws need not be arbitrary or immutable, to be blindly followed or as blindly opposed, but can be creative approaches to felt needs, flexible and open to change in an orderly process.

Assignments. The teacher can ask each citizen of a block town, village, city, or other community to carry out a specific task in a given period of time. Young children may be asked to visit one friend or to go to two forms of entertainment during a block period. Older children may have more complex assignments: getting a law passed; procuring the raw materials for a manufacturing enterprise; interviewing citizens or government officials for a newspaper article—all within the confines of their block city.

Regardless of age, children who are beginning their experience with blocks go through developmental stages (see Appendix 1). Elementary-level children quickly reach—or have already attained—conceptual ability and skill in representing the real world with blocks, as with other materials. The teacher will want to see children using increasingly rigorous standards of reality, incorporating more detail, including clearer sequential and logical representations of processes, and incorporating into their miniworld indications of more abstract interrelationships. Children in the early elementary years are still moving out of an egocentric position. The teacher can look for and support children's efforts to take into account another's viewpoint—for example, "How will people in the city know about the shoe sale?"

Children in the upper elementary grades are moving toward more formal logical thinking. They are increasingly able to find symbolic ways to represent ideas and relationships. They may make judgments about the salient features of their city, abstract essential qualities, generate keys and other symbolic representations, and create constructions that are models and three-dimensional mappings. Preadolescent children are approaching a time when they can consider hypothetical situations and can be expected to demonstrate a beginning ability to draw on what they have learned about the real world to construct a "what-if" world and explore its implications. This is another example of the way in which concrete experience with blocks supports the growth of facility and power in dealing with abstractions.

The teacher selects the kind of structure the group needs for a variety of purposes: to promote interaction, to extend learning, to raise a question, to clarify thinking, to generate new interest, or to pose new problems for their consideration. Children give us cues concerning their interests, needs, misconceptions, and areas of readiness. Sometimes the most important time the teacher spends in block period is the time spent quietly observing the children at work.

As children work in the block area, they are building—in addition to cities, towns, rivers, and bridges—an inner map of their world. They are building a view of learning in which finding that something doesn't work is not a failure but a cue to think and try again. They are learning the value of their own ideas and the courage to test them. They are learning the value of the ideas of others and the confidence to consider them. Blocks have the flexibility that invites imagination and the structure that requires respect. They afford children opportunities that characterize the best education: the chance to venture and to reflect, to convince and to compromise, to wonder and to know, to reason and to dream.

References

Bearison, D. 1982. New directions in studies of social interaction and cognitive growth. In *Social cognitive development in context*, ed. F. Serafica. New York: Guilford.

Bobrow, D.G., & A.M. Collins, eds. 1975. *Representation and understanding: Studies in cognitive science.* New York: Academic.

Bransford, J.D., J. Barclay, & J. Franks. 1972. Sentence memory: A constructive versus an interpretive approach. *Cognitive Psychology* 3: 193–210.

Bransford, J.D., & N.S. McCarrell. 1974. A sketch of a cognitive approach to comprehension: Some thoughts about understanding what it means to comprehend. In *Cognition and the symbolic processes*, eds. W.B. Weimer & D.S. Palermo. Hillsdale, NJ: Erlbaum.

Kintsch, W., & T.A. Van Dijk. 1978. Toward a model of text comprehension and production. *Psychological Review* 84 (5): 363–94.

Piaget, J. 1955. *The child's construction of reality.* London: Routledge & Kegan Paul.

Piaget, J., & B. Inhelder. 1969. *The psychology of the child.* London: Routledge & Kegan Paul.

Rumelhart, D., & A. Ortory. 1977. The representation of knowledge in memory. In *Schooling and the acquisition of knowledge*, eds. R. Anderson, R. Spiro, & W. Montague. Hillsdale, NJ: Erlbaum.

8

Block Building:
Practical Considerations for
the Classroom Teacher

Elisabeth S. Hirsch

Contributors to this volume have examined the various *whys* of block-building activity. The practitioner, however, needs a *how* in addition to the *why*. This chapter endeavors to relate theory to practice.

The physical space

Good education begins before the first child enters the classroom. The allocation of space, physical proximity or distance between activities, flow of traffic, and selection and display of materials all influence children and their learning environment.

Room arrangement

Nowhere is the adage "environment speaks to children" more appropriate than in relation to physical space available for block-building activities. Block building needs a great deal of room. In an average classroom, about one third of the floor space should be available for blocks. Adjoining, moveable shelves and dividers can be pushed against the wall to make more room.

Of course, such space can be used for many other purposes at one time or another. It can be used for circle time by moving chairs or cushions. Certainly the block area can be put to use for music rhythm activities, so if there is a piano, placing it next to the block area makes sense. The area also can be used at other times. At mealtime, tables and chairs that were pushed to the side or stacked during activity periods will easily find a place in the large block area. At naptime, cots can occupy the space.

Block building requires a great deal of room.

Environment speaks to children. If a room is cluttered with tables (or desks) and chairs, it says, "I want you to sit still and control your urge to explore and to interact with people and things." If the room is too large and undivided (like some church halls and gymnasiums), it says, "Run!" Children in such environments often feel abandoned. They miss supportive adult control. Their hysterical behavior shows that inner tensions have risen. It is difficult to achieve constructive, growth-promoting activities in rooms that are either too crowded or cavernously spacious.

The block area should be large enough to provide room to build for all children who wish to do so. It is also desirable to have this area open, visible from other parts of the room. Fascinating patterns of interaction can develop between dramatic play areas, table toy areas, science areas, and the block corner.

In selecting the best area for blocks, teachers must consider the total traffic pattern. Block areas should be away from cross-traffic caused by the proximity of entrance doors or the bathroom.

In planning room arrangements, experienced teachers usually select the block area *first*; the rest of the room will then be easy to arrange. The diagram on p. 119 of a floor plan shows one satisfactory solution.

Classrooms where the block area is too small or insufficiently equipped force teachers to restrict the numbers of children participating in block activities. This seems rather regrettable, not only because of the arbitrariness of the narrowed choices but because it may imply that children assigned to block play will have to stay in that area during the free play period. Children should have free movement whenever possible. Adjoining areas ought to provide cross-fertilization of ideas and populations. Involvement and attention length can only develop under conditions of free choice and commitment. When an area does become overpopulated, teachers could move furniture to accommodate children who are interested in the activity area. The aim of a well-arranged room should be a flow of activities that allows movement of children from one activity to another as their interest is piqued or if they lose interest in what they are doing. If the room is arranged in such a way that the housekeeping area, for example, is near the block area, the resulting interchange often enriches dramatic play in both areas.

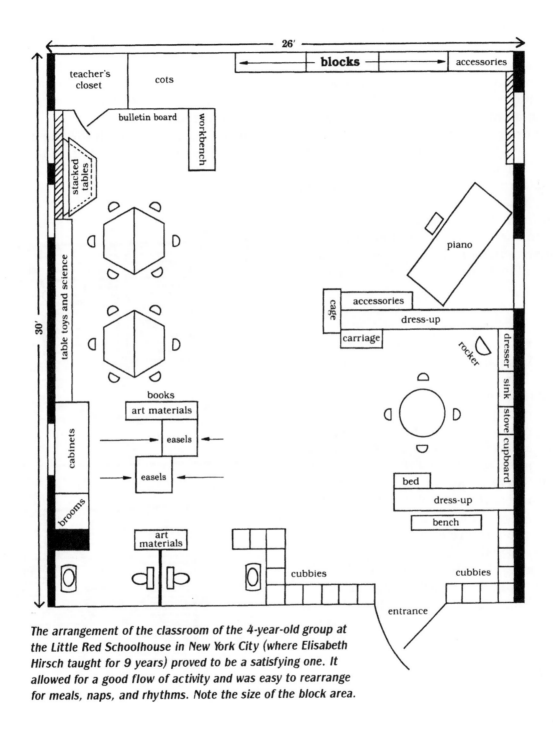

The arrangement of the classroom of the 4-year-old group at the Little Red Schoolhouse in New York City (where Elisabeth Hirsch taught for 9 years) proved to be a satisfying one. It allowed for a good flow of activity and was easy to rearrange for meals, naps, and rhythms. Note the size of the block area.

Flooring

Any good, even flooring, free of splinters and away from drafts, is suitable for block building. Indoor/outdoor carpets (no pile) are certainly an attractive luxury in this area, as in any other part of the classroom. However, they are not vital—it should not be necessary to muffle the noise of falling blocks! A constructive classroom is a noisy place. Of course, accidents do happen and buildings do collapse, but in classes where children pile blocks upon each other just to knock them down, constructive block activity does not exist. More about this later.

Shelving

Blocks need a great deal of shelf space. Three or four shelf units, each approximately 4 feet wide, 3 feet high, and 1 foot deep, containing three shelves each, are probably the minimum required. Less space will cause crowding (provided sufficient blocks and accessories are available) and make the blocks uninviting; more is certainly desirable. Shelving does not have to be expensive. Any handy carpenter can create good block shelves. (See Appendix 2 for specific suggestions for shelving.) Many teachers prefer not to have shelves attached to the walls. Judicious rearrangement of rooms, often the best remedy for midyear doldrums, is more easily accomplished with movable shelves. Movable shelves also can be used as room dividers wherever necessary. If some of the shelves have vertical subdivisions, they will encourage neater placement of various shapes and of accessories.

Arrangement on shelves

Environment speaks to children. If blocks on shelves are too neatly arranged, they say, "Don't touch"; if they are too messy, they fail to suggest satisfying activity. What is "too neat"? A shelf filled with identical blocks from top to bottom, back to front, is too neat.

This is too neat!

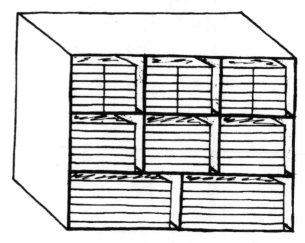

This is also too neat!

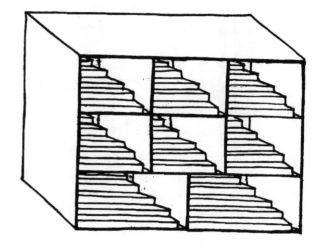

A shelf with identical blocks, on which the bottom row reaches the front and the rest recede in irregular steps, and from which the removal of a block does not destroy the entire design, is, on the other hand, inviting.

A shelf on which units or double units are arranged so that the narrow ends face outward will be uninviting for another reason: builders will not be able to differentiate easily between half-units, units, and double units. The children will be prevented from purposeful selection that furthers their work. Moreover, they will not be able to benefit from seeing the mathematical relationships between the sizes of blocks, as discussed in chapter 4, "The Block Builder Mathematician."

What is "too messy"? Unfortunately, messy shelves are all too common and hence need no description. They compare to a purposefully arranged block area in the same way as a box full of tools thrown in helter-skelter compares to a workshop where the worker can reach neatly arranged tools without a laborious search. Block carts, boxes on wheels featured in many catalogs, invite the jumble just described and are not recommended.

Shelf arrangements may be kept neat easily, if the shapes that belong in each space are indicated on the shelf in some way. Shapes can be painted on shelves. They may be traced on plain adhesive-backed paper (such as Contact Paper) of a contrasting color and pasted on the shelf. Miniature shapes on the outside edge of the shelf itself might be helpful to older children. But younger children might not be able to grasp the one-to-one correlation when the size of the representation differs from the actual size of the block.

The blocks

Sizes and shapes

Although Caroline Pratt failed to patent the blocks she designed, manufacturers fortunately retain the proportions and sizes of the original unit blocks. The following measurements are expressed in inches.

Children can more easily keep shelves neat if shapes belonging in each space are indicated in some way; shapes may be traced on adhesive-backed paper and stuck to the shelves or simply be painted on.

The *basic unit* is a brick-shaped rectangle ($1^3/_8$ x $2^3/_4$ x $5^1/_2$). The *half unit* is square ($1^3/_8$ x $2^3/_4$ x $2^3/_4$). The *double unit* is $1^3/_8$ x $2^3/_4$ x 11. The *quadruple unit* measures $1^3/_8$ x $2^3/_4$ x 22. In addition to these basic shapes, there are quarter units, triangles, ramps formed by bisecting a half unit, and other shapes.

There is a great variety of other blocks combining straight and round surfaces, such as arches, pillars, and cylinders of various sorts. These provide additional stimuli to block-building activities. Appendix 2 contains a recommended list of blocks for each age group.

Care of blocks

Blocks are expensive. They are usually the most expensive equipment besides furniture. With good care, blocks should last at least 10 years before they begin to splinter. Sanding can extend their life even further.

Blocks should be made of hardwood, usually elm or maple. Softwood blocks are not durable enough for schools. They are too light and thus topple easily. They dent and splinter sooner and, in the long run, are more expensive.

Blocks will last if they are kept dry and free of dust. During long vacations, blocks can be kept in boxes or on their original shelves masked with newspapers or plastic. Occasional oiling, waxing, or shellacking will prolong block life considerably. This is a job that may be done by teachers and children together. In addition to practical considerations, such an activity also will convey to children an attitude of appreciation for this material. Needless to say, blocks should not be used for other activities, for example, in lieu of a hammer in woodwork, instead of a rolling pin with clay, in conjunction with water or sand, or as a doorstop.

Accessories

Accessories are indispensable to block activities. They can add stimulation, variety, beauty, and dramatic play content to block play.

The most useful accessories are *human and animal figures*. These figures may be made of wood, plastic, rubber, or other materials. Other accessories include *cars, planes, boats, buses, trucks*—the list is virtually endless. Many of these items are readily available. Safety factors must be taken into consideration, of course. Sharp-edged tiny pieces can cause cuts and scratches. Soft cars (rubber or plastic) with the wheels attached to rigid metal axles present another safety hazard. When knelt on, the axles can cause puncture wounds, for instance.

Interconnecting trains and interconnecting blocks are often popular and useful accessories.

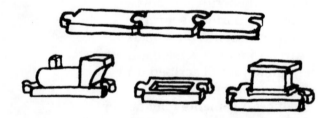

Another type of accessories is *decorations*. A finished building can gain further interest when the teacher suggests that it could be decorated. (See Appendix 2 for lists of accessories and suggestions for inexpensive and found materials that can enrich block play.)

It is worthwhile to note here that while accessories may be brightly colored, blocks should remain unpainted. Experiments with colored blocks have shown that they tend to restrict rather than stimulate imaginative activity.

A wise teacher does not display all accessories at one time. At the beginning of the year, such wealth may be overwhelming. Reserves are necessary to pick up activities when they lag around mid-year. There also should be a reserve available to enrich special interests as they occur. Some odd-shaped blocks might also be kept for later in the year.

Other building materials

In many schools, large building materials are kept for outdoor use. Wooden hollow blocks and packing cases, ladders, sawhorses, cleated boards, etc. are standard equipment of many preschool playyards. If space permits, large-scale equipment adds an interesting further dimension to indoor play, enriching role playing and other dramatic play.

Relatively inexpensive hollow blocks made of corrugated board are usually reinforced inside and can easily support the weight of a child. These blocks have many uses. They can extend dramatic play activities by providing child-size props. Their main disadvantage is that they are too light for high construction. There are other adverse features to consider. Cardboard blocks have a colorful patterned exterior, which prevents

Painting or taping a line on the floor shows children how far from the shelf their constructions must be to allow other children to get more blocks.

rather than stimulates imaginative use. This exterior surface soon becomes shabby and worn looking. The blocks lack what Harriet Cuffaro calls the "unitary harmonious nature of blocks" (see chapter 6). For a full discussion of hollow blocks, see chapter 9.

Teacher concerns

The most important resource in the classroom, of course, is the teacher. Like a giant Gulliver, the teacher is an ever-present influence, constantly watched by the little Lilliputians. Teacher understanding, support, and skill can help children feel secure and at ease. Only then can they benefit from the carefully arranged environment.

Beginning activities

Parents who expect preschoolers to play with children their own age are always amazed when they watch beginning block activities. Children build side by side, seemingly unaware of the presence of others. This is parallel play, a mode of activity that marks the beginning of block play at all ages and does not last long. Children soon become aware of the helpful or disturbing presence of others. At this point, when social codes have not yet emerged, when the activity does not yet provide real satisfaction, and when adjustment-time anxiety is high, teachers have to be especially aware of the block area. It is inevitable for young children first entering a group to become frustrated easily. It is, therefore, doubly necessary for the environment (including the teacher) to exert a calming influence. Teacher movement preferably should not be rushed or sudden. Shrill or tense teacher voices affect children.

The building area should be neat and calming. This is not yet the time to teach habits of neatness. Some disarray is unavoidable in the beginning: blocks will be scattered; buildings will remain half-finished or will collapse; the area will take on a disorderly, uninviting appearance. It is wisest at this time, while the children are still busy, for adults to pick up these uninviting (and hazardous) eyesores. Good cleanup habits will be easier to promote after playtime is over for the day.

Some preventive measures are also in order at this time. Without fail, children begin their buildings too close to each other or to the shelves. Moving the building to a safe spot is probably more effective at this point than trying to enforce rules. Painting or taping a line on the floor shows children how far from the shelf their construction must be to allow other children to get more blocks.

The first limitations to be introduced should probably have to do with respect for the activity itself—and for other people: "No, we mustn't knock down buildings. Let me help you take yours down." "It is dangerous to drive cars into buildings." "I can't let you throw blocks." No matter how we try to limit it, beginning group life is full of no-nos.

Role of the teacher

What if children don't use the blocks? Teachers often feel tempted to start building themselves, providing models. This, however, can lead to imitation and discouragement. Children, moreover, must follow their own timetable and proceed stage by stage (see Appendix 1). There are, however, a number of simple techniques that might encourage block play.

Satisfying, ongoing activities do not require teacher presence. Teachers can calmly circulate while remaining aware of potential disturbances or hazards. A teacher's presence, though, may prove inviting and reassuring. A teacher sitting quietly in the block area soon has a number of builders around, especially in the early weeks of the school year. Another practice is derived from Gestalt psychology, which teaches us that people are bothered by unfinished tasks. Placing two double units at right angles in a conspicuous spot on the floor usually provokes some sort of block activity.

But the most important facilitator, of course, is the teacher's attitude. Teachers who value block building will find verbal and nonverbal ways of transmitting those values. These teachers will be available when children have to share blocks. They will suggest a good place for building. Good teachers will provide moral support for fumbling artists. They will give suggestions, such as building a house or garage for a favorite toy or pet. They will ask challenging questions. They will stay with beginners, praise experimenters, and protect (or occasionally reconstruct) buildings. The activity (the process) is valued over the finished building (the product).

Setting limits and standards

The teacher's role includes all facets of preventive safety. Sooner or later some rules have to be introduced—and repeated. Presenting beginning builders with a list of no-nos might be a mistake, of course. It is usually more effective to step in quietly but promptly, making quite clear that certain actions are not acceptable.

• Remove blocks from the shelf only as needed.

• Do not walk on blocks (it is dangerous).

• Never throw blocks.

• Keep block buildings far enough from the shelf (1 to 3 feet) to allow other children to get more blocks (painting or taping a line on the floor often helps to indicate the limit).

• Limit the height of buildings—this differs by child age and experience, as well as by what teachers think children can handle, but limits should be clearly understood.

• Do not knock, push, or kick down buildings.

Let us remember, though, that rules are made to help us, not to enslave us! There are times for exceptions to every rule. Children mature, teachers become more confident, individuals have differing needs. Children do not hold precedents against us. It is wise to avoid overreaction to infractions—better to be guided by the needs of the children.

Collapsing buildings (accidental or otherwise), for instance, evoke panic reactions from children. They often throw themselves upon the pile with swimming movements. They seem completely overcome and, if no adult help is available *at once*, the sense of hysteria and "hyper" feelings can lead to even more loss of self-control. Many teachers in such a situation find that if they step in rapidly and pile identical-size blocks three to four high right there on the floor, then the children will relax, carry the piles to the shelves, or even use them for new buildings then and there. The environment that seemed so threatening a few seconds before has become inviting again.

Once activities are well established and buildings become complex, the problem arises of whether or not to leave buildings up. There is no simple answer to this question once practical considerations, such as multiple use of space, do not interfere. The answer probably depends on the effect of leaving up the buildings. Does it convey to the children a respect for their effort? Does it stimulate extension, addition, improvement, decoration, or dramatic activity? Does it stimulate others to extend themselves by its example and by the appreciation of the adult? Or, conversely, does it discourage others, monopolize too much space, or use up so many blocks that there are not enough left for further activity? (In the latter case, does this class need more blocks?) Sometimes children clamor to leave a building up, but by the next day they have lost interest. They are not yet ready for such an extended effort.

In rooms where buildings cannot be left up because the space is needed for another activity or another group, teachers sometimes have to help children over the heartbreak of dismantling. A sketch or a Polaroid picture of a beloved building will convey adult appreciation, as well as provide permanency to an impermanent structure. Such pictures might serve as a basis for rebuilding the following day. They also can be exhibited for children and adults to admire.

Certainly no building should be left up because it is too much trouble to clear away.

Scheduling time for block building and cleanup

To be satisfying and successful, block building needs a sufficient amount of time. One hour seems to be the minimum amount that children will need to have a satisfying building experience and time for cleanup. Providing the time can be accomplished by allowing all free-choice activities to occur at the same time, including table activities and construction projects. Giving children many simultaneous choices also will reduce crowding in block and dramatic play areas.

The one-hour guideline is not a hard-and-fast rule, however. Beginners and very young children, not fully absorbed in building, need less time. Experienced and sophisticated block builders may find one hour very restrictive. The average classroom schedule, however, is usually hemmed in by mealtimes and outdoor periods that, unfortunately, necessitate the reduction of free play time.

Rainy days often offer welcome opportunities for extended free play periods. Some teachers have found that they can serve breakfast or snack on a self-help buffet basis without the need for prior cleanup, allowing children to serve themselves and then return to ongoing activities.

Cleanup time has to be considered when scheduling time for block play. Ten minutes seems to be sufficient for the average preschool block cleanup. Less time will be needed for beginners. Much more time and several reminders will be required for children involved in complex constructions.

Some teachers sing a "cleanup song" or give a prearranged signal (such as a chord on the piano) that suddenly announces cleanup time. At the beginning of the year or in classes where the children's involvement level is low this probably is quite effective, but for serious, involved builders, putting an immediate end to their activities is a frustra-

Cleanup should be a purposeful, satisfying activity in its own right.

Teacher respect for individual activity, moreover, is better expressed with personal or small group reminders. Length of time for cleanup must be carefully scheduled and varied as the complexity of building activities increases. Cleanup time should be nonrushed and leisurely—it should not lead to inactivity and boredom.

Some teachers place themselves in front of the block shelves and have children "deliver" various blocks to them. Other teachers pile up blocks in the way described in the Setting Limits and Standards section.

In some classes, cleanup time seems like a recurring nightmare to teachers; in others, it is a purposeful, busy activity enjoyed by all. How do we avoid the former and achieve the latter? It is necessary to consider some of the dynamics that cause difficulties during cleanup periods.

Anxiety is an important consideration. While anxiety in minute quantities acts as a spur to investigative and creative activities, its destructive potential is enormous. A satisfying and busy activity period provides sufficient support to keep anxiety at bay. But transitions of any kind remove this support, and anxiety rears its destructive head. This issue is discussed more fully in *Transition Periods: Stumbling Blocks of Education* (Hirsch n.d.). Feelings of insecurity, homesickness, and aggression surface; inner

tion too hard to bear. Serious builders need to be reminded several times, well ahead, to finish up, because soon it will be cleanup time. The frequency of reminders will vary with groups, age levels, and individuals.

127

controls decrease. To alleviate these feelings, teachers can follow certain guidelines:

• Cleanup should be a purposeful, satisfying activity in its own right, with enough time allowed for it to prevent rushing.

• Children need a future orientation, i.e., they need to know what activity follows cleanup.

• Confusion and destruction should be kept to a minimum. Knowing where the blocks go provides children with a feeling of security. Having a teacher hand down the blocks from the upper story of a high building, thus avoiding collapse, prevents destructiveness. So does the quick response described earlier, should a building topple.

• Waiting or inactivity makes anxiety rise. No child should be kept waiting at any time during transition periods, even if this means that some have snacks or go outdoors before everyone has completed cleanup. Children should know where to go once they are finished.

• Clear expectation of purposeful activity and a follow-through by actively participating teachers eliminate children's feelings of helplessness.

• Teacher help (and presence) also makes the task seem more manageable and more worthwhile.

There are number of further points to consider. In some schools the expectation is that "Everybody cleans up their own messes." Apart from the fact that important activities cannot be designated as "messes," we have a further pitfall here: It is certainly easier to clean up some crayons and paper than to disassemble an enormous block building. Block builders will soon assume that they are being punished. Block activity will fade. It is easier, then, to expect help from everyone in all areas to clean up *our* room. For some children, helping at cleanup provides their first acquaintance with blocks.

The enjoyment of cleanup as an activity in its own right will be enhanced if children have wagons and carts to use in delivering the blocks to the shelves. Some children pile the blocks onto chairs and push them to the shelves. If the area looks confused, teachers or children can pile up the blocks in twos or threes to reduce confusion. In one school, a teacher introduced first-graders to mathematical sets by announcing that "Today we will put the blocks away in sets of two (or three or four)." Cleanup of this sort will produce its own patterns of cooperation and specialization; thus, important social factors are at work. Of course, teachers can and should be part of the team also!

Even children who enjoy cleaning up may begin building again while piling blocks on carts or chairs for delivery. The material is, after all, just too enticing! Teachers will have to use their own judgment about how to handle this in a not-too-discouraging way.

Just as in any other activity, children will test limits during cleanup. Here again, teachers must use individual judgment in dealing with children's behavior. We have to differentiate between testing and genuine need to do a little less on occasion. A hard-working builder might simply be too tired to clean up. Fatigue might be caused by other, less immediate reasons as well. Certainly cleanup should never seem like a punishment, but neither should those who enjoy it feel that they have been had!

Because cleanup is often followed by toileting and washing hands, the two activities can go on simultaneously. Children can return from the bathroom to help further, if necessary. Such a flexible arrangement gives an easy "out" to tired block builders, without a clash of wills and bad feelings.

Other teacher concerns

Teachers are often concerned by the quality of the building activity. Some groups don't seem to graduate from creating flat, two-dimensional outlines to genuine building. Some groups repeat other simple patterns seemingly forever. There is no single solution for either of these problems, because they often come from a variety of sources. Social leadership can be one cause—the most admired and imitated block builder is not always the most imaginative one. On the other hand, more mature or experienced builders provide effective inspiration, as illustrated in the video *A Classroom with Blocks* (Berlfein 1987). Teachers must, therefore, be aware of and, if necessary, alter social constellations or further other potential ideas. Sometimes this is the time for introducing some new accessories or for taking the group on an interesting trip.

The length of the initial block-building period and the style of building can vary with the previous experience of the children. Urban children will build differently from rural ones. Native American children will need to re-create experiences that differ widely from those of children in the hills of Appalachia. And many children of our "TV generation" are more accustomed to passive intake than active construction.

Another problem is posed by "tippy" buildings. Equilibrium, balance, and stability are discussed in chapter 3, "Children Learn about Science through Block Building." It would be relatively easy to point out how buildings can be made more stable, but learning through problem solving will have more depth if children discover solutions themselves. Teachers will find that wise questioning often promotes better learning than showing how. Of course, teachers sometimes have to give a hint or help with a technical problem and not worry that they have stifled the child's thinking forever.

Children's concerns

Block building, like any other important satisfying activity, helps children gain skill in social relationships. Some children seem to have a natural endowment in this respect, while others face a very hard time. Teachers can help children with poor social skills by giving them specific suggestions on good ways to enter activities, such as, "Have you tried to bring them something they need for their building, like this horse?" Teacher disapproval of social discrimination can be conveyed in many ways and will discourage such practices.

In some classes, the block area seems to be a boy's domain and the housekeeping area that of the girls. Neither practice is rooted in children's nature, as is clearly evidenced in classes where this segregation does not exist. Again, teacher attitudes can convey that *all* children can enjoy these activities.

Aggression and destruction

Adults often are concerned about aggressive children in the block area. Certainly, children have to be made clearly aware of dos and

Teachers need to convey that blocks are fun for girls and boys alike.

don'ts in relation to the blocks themselves. The reward in satisfaction gleaned from block building is so great, however, that blocks are hardly ever used as weapons. Children with extremely weak inner controls have to be very carefully watched, of course, and removed from the area, if necessary. Some people think that such children should be allowed to knock down buildings, etc., for the emotional release this activity provides. Such an activity, while appropriate in a play-therapy situation, is inappropriate and misplaced in a school. Schools should address themselves to personality strengths, which they try to nurture and foster. Teachers can provide children who have weak inner controls with the control they lack by providing and enforcing safety rules. Impulsive or fearful children often can be helped in this way to feel safe, protected, and able to benefit from school activities. Most aggressive children relax and become less threatening once they feel safe. Safety, for them, means a teacher who protects them from their own impulsivity, as well as from outside threats, even if the protection means their removal from the block area.

Children who bump into buildings, whether by accident or on purpose, are more common. They, too, need to be told that they are not yet ready to play in the block area, and after a lapse of time, they can re-enter on probation—"Are you ready to be more careful now?" Such accidents will occur less often if buildings are kept about five feet apart. Children who have such accidents may have problems relating to space perception or body image. Large-muscle activities, such as those involving balancing, are especially important for such children.

Noise

While purposeful, quiet play is much to be desired, a busy classroom is almost always a noisy place. Voices rise in the excitement and stimulation of activities and, alas, blocks can tumble noisily even with careful handling. Because this is part of the growth and learning-promoting way children interact with materials, insisting on hushed "indoor voices" in an early childhood classroom seems futile.

Experienced teachers know how to differentiate between "good noise" and "bad noise." Although both kinds of noise are sometimes rather loud, "bad noise" has a hysterical, "hyper" quality. The secret of teachers "seeing with the backs of their heads" is that they *hear* the changed higher pitch in children's voices and go to the affected area immediately. Very often the teacher's presence alone provides enough reassurance, and children will relax; at other times, the teacher may have to take other action of an appropriate nature.

Blocks and language

Some children are eager to discuss their buildings and explain various features. Teachers should encourage this discussion, of course, because language adds another dimension to the block-building activity—a better ability to apply their learnings at another time. Teachers who are sure they know what children mean to express also may supply missing vocabulary. As soon as children have obtained the concept (the idea) but lack the *label*, a new word will help them to remember and to talk about their construction. "I see you made a ramp" provides a child with the new word *ramp*. Talking about buildings becomes superficial and artificial and can interfere with the process itself, if children are *expected* to describe their buildings. Avoid asking a child *what is it?* It's much better to ask the child whether she wants to *tell about it*. Pointing out to the other children some special features, such as secure foundations, interesting ramps, etc., will gratify the builder, stimulate others, and build vocabulary.

Evaluation

The emphasis of this chapter is on process rather than on product. Learning and growth processes are induced through the block-building activity.

How, then, can a concerned teacher evaluate activity in a classroom? How does the teacher know that an endeavor was successful? that children gain optimum benefit from block-building activities?

The answer lies not in the *what* of block building but in the *how*. If children work with an intensity that denotes satisfaction, we must be on the right track. What we are looking for is self-investment that encompasses the whole body, all senses, the intellect as well as the emotions.

Children just beginning their acquaintance with blocks are never fully involved. They are what one teacher called "hit-and-run builders." Cleanup time for them is a five-minute affair requiring no advance notice.

As the satisfaction provided by the material itself has an effect, things change. You can tell that children are involved by the noise quality in the room; there is a low, satisfied, busy hum in the block corner. You can see the children's intensity by touching or looking at their backs: there is a purposeful readying of muscles—this is not harmful tension, nor is it bored lassitude; this is a body at work. Look at children's faces. Happy, busy block builders belie the stereotyped image of childhood: they don't laugh, they don't even smile—they are serious workers.

This is the point at which the teacher who structured the room and the block area, who used psychology and diplomacy, who learned to bend and to kneel, to limit and to cajole, reaps the rewards. Block building is worth it!

References

Berlfein, J., prod. 1987. *A classroom with blocks*. 13 min. Washington, DC: NAEYC. Videocassette.

Hirsch, E. n.d. *Transition periods: Stumbling blocks of education*. New York: New York City Association for the Education of Young Children.

9

Learning with Large Blocks

Sally Cartwright

Every day, teachers and parents see children learning through their own invention, involvement, and discovery, much as they learn to walk and talk. And to learn a thing well means to experience and use it. We know that young children are more physical than verbal, and we know that children's creative dramatic play is a valuable way of learning. It is not surprising, then, that large hollow blocks meet many child learning needs. As we shall see in this chapter, they spark the vision, warmth, and energy of the whole child.

More than 70 years ago, Caroline Pratt, with the help of a pediatrician, first developed these large blocks to give young children safe, comprehensive exercise for their arms and shoulders. But Pratt, with her intuitive insight and keen observation, soon found that the children not only loved to build structures that they could climb into and over, developing their strength, coordi-

nation, balance and self-esteem; they also shared—and often disputed!—information about the world around them. They built houses, stores, factories, barns, bridges, and boats. As they put their thinking to real use,

With large blocks children build structures they can climb into and over; they build their own world in which to explore and live and understand.

133

they discovered relationships, the sinews of knowing. Not only were the young builders solving construction problems together, they also became moms, dads, animals, cooks, drivers, farmers, fishing crews, and mill workers. With their whole beings they played out fantasy and real-life situations, learning with mind, muscle, and heart. Copying the real world, they built their own world in which to explore and live and understand.

The importance of well-made blocks

Large hollow blocks, boards, and packing boxes, often with small ladders and sawhorses (see Figure 1), are designed to fit each other for accurate, safe building, not to mention down-to-earth experience in solid geometry. The blocks, boards, and sawhorses also fit the arms of young builders. They are light enough to carry yet sturdy enough to support children's weight and bustle. It is wise to provide well-made equipment to show the children that their learning endeavor is appreciated. For this reason, cardboard boxes and other flimsy materials should not be used.

Since parents and teachers, as amateur carpenters, can make all this equipment (see Figure 2), the cost is relatively low, while rewards for learning are high. Neatly cut, glued, nailed, and with corners and end grains well sanded, the blocks will lift your children's self-esteem and invite their affectionate use and care. The good feelings that children have because "Dad, Mom, and my teacher made these for us" are indeed powerful.

Alone, the blocks represent nothing but simple, rectangular shapes; child imagination and hard work can transform them into

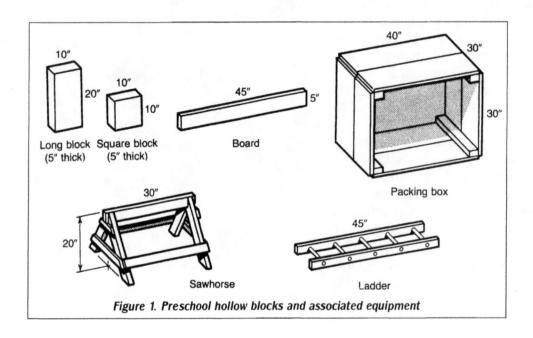

Figure 1. Preschool hollow blocks and associated equipment

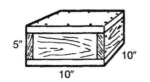

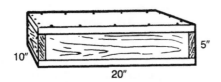

Materials: White pine, #2 grade (make sure knots are tight and solid)

Apply three coats of nongloss polyurethane.

Rough-sand broad surfaces to prevent blocks from slipping when stacked.

2½" galvanized finishing nails

Waterproof glue

Nail and glue sides first. Nail and glue top and bottom onto this frame, fully enclosing the block. Top and bottom extend to outer edges.

Roofing boards, 1" x 5" x 40", and packing boxes, 30" x 30" x 40", may be constructed of pine to fit these blocks.

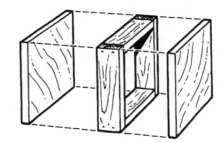

Note: Designed by Sally Cartwright from Pratt originals at City & Country School. Copyright © 1979 by Sally Cartwright, Community Nursery School, Tenants Harbor, ME 04860.

Figure 2. Hollow blocks for early childhood

inventive group constructions—from kitchens to spaceships. The size and three-dimensional boldness of these structures represent mastery. One day I watched Jeannie lugging big blocks across the work area to build her airplane. The action itself was contagious. Bill asked to join her.

"OK," she said. "Get those boards and make the wings."

"What are *you* making?"

"These are seats, stupid, It's a Boeing 707, and it's going to crash."

"No, it's not!" I shot in, laughing. "You can build better than that."

"You bet!" agreed these young engineers with a confidence and deep satisfaction that made my day.

Where and when

During cold winters, like those we have in Maine, indoors is the best setting for large block play. Children can choose to work with large blocks during an open-choice morning that also includes easel painting, clay, unit blocks, and so on. A 10' x 12' area with firm carpet provides sufficient room for up to eight young builders. In a preschool, about 20 blocks (10 long and 10 square) with 10 boards is adequate; at home, 10 to 20 blocks will do. Because all the blocks will be used, the emphasis is on dramatic play. Building with large blocks should be clearly separate from unit block building. The two activities should not be mixed.

When we teachers have the courage to use it effectively, there is ample space for large hollow blocks in the classroom. These blocks can *replace* domestic-play furniture, freeing floor space for dramatic play with the children's own constructions. The removal of adult-designed equipment invites the children's own creative initiative, allowing them to build just what *they* need, whether it be a house, fire station, plane or boat. Because the play is not steered by, say, a stove or a sink, it becomes less repetitive and more inviting to the children. With well-planned group trips and bountiful reading aloud, children's building turns truly inventive.

Indoor large blocks should be stored by size along a wall or partition adjacent to the play area. One needs far fewer large blocks indoors than out. They're all in use in minutes, so the indoor emphasis is less on building and more on dramatic play. Often the blocks truly become, in the child's own style, *suggestive* representations of reality. When steered by their own learning purpose,

how well these young children can adapt to immediate circumstance!

Outdoors, more elaborate building and consequent learning can take place. Packing boxes, ladders, wagons, small freight dollies, and small sawhorses can be added to the blocks. Level space, the equivalent of roughly 30' x 40', with three to five times as many blocks and boards as are used indoors and at least two packing boxes, will stimulate good building and play. In the spring, summer, and fall, preschool programs can offer wonderful outdoor learning with large blocks.

Indoors, with a limited quantity of large blocks and building space, children tend to use blocks more for dramatic-play purposes than for elaborate building.

Indoor and outdoor large-block programs complement each other. Often, when the children can go out in warmer weather, they carry their play themes with them, build more fully, and attract more children and ideas into their play.

Respect for children's active learning suggests that they be allowed to pursue activities in their own ways the moment they enter the classroom. Preschoolers, especially, are workers, not talkers, and need no discussion before launching into their morning endeavor, be it an individual or group venture. Children should be able to choose and change activities at will without verbal planning. This approach, in a cooperative atmosphere of warmth, humor, and hard work, tells the children that their own choice and discovery are valuable.

When children build according to their own needs, rich dramatic play ensues, particularly when well-chosen accessories are readily available. Again, it is wise to avoid structured materials and toys. Indoors, instead of costumes, children should use variously shaped, sized, and textured pieces of cloth with well-placed strips of Velcro. Instead of representational toys and hardware, teachers can provide an abundant assortment of small unit blocks (*only* for accessories, not for building), which become cups, telephones, tools, sandwiches, machinery, flight controls—whatever. Outdoors, twigs, pebbles, sand, pails, and wood scraps make fine accessories. Indoors and out, a few 4-foot lengths of quarter-inch rope, each with an eye spliced in one end, are wonderful additions, but the rule "No rope around necks" must be firmly enforced. Crayons, paper, and masking tape should be handy because children often need to make signs for their play.

Trust in children's inventiveness

If we parents and teachers rely largely on prestructured play activities that use representational toys and equipment, they may need courage to trust children's ingenuity, creative energy, and persistence. Needless to say, an observant adult must be on hand at all times to ensure physical and emotional safety. With blocks and accessories, children make all the learning materials they need for dramatic play and grow from the experience. Jeannie's airplane is a case in point. More children joined Jeannie in the project. (The group not only had been to the Rockland airport, they also had climbed aboard to explore a plane at the Owls Head Transportation Museum.) Jeannie made her seats. Carl made tickets. Nancy constructed the pilot's cab and argued hotly with Josh about the controls. She finally said,

"Oh, go help Bill with the wings. This is a jet, after all."

That somehow ended the matter, and Josh was soon criticizing Bill.

"You forgot the jet engines."

"Can't. The whole thing's gonna fall over."

"You could put one under each wing, like in the book," suggested Molly, who, as usual, had stood watching before working. Bill and Josh looked at each other, nodded, and set to work.

Later, as the boys surveyed their workmanship, I heard Josh admit, "Molly's not so dumb."

Perhaps Josh felt good enough about his work with Bill to doff a bit of honest credit elsewhere. In any case, as he took part in this sort of play he gradually became less conten-

Creating their own play environments with large blocks, children feel a sense of group ownership and caring seldom found in play with prestructured equipment.

tious and more open to the ideas of others. Children, working together intently, learn to listen to and watch each other, respect differences, and value inventive contributions from the group. From trips, discussion, and the teacher's reading aloud, they gather and use information for their own purpose. Here is not only budding democracy but effective learning.

Benefits to children

With large hollow blocks, children can shape their own learning environments. This gives them a sense of group ownership and caring

seldom found in prestructured play. For example, these blocks ask miniature moms and dads to design and build their own domestic play space and equipment, a creative task of active, cooperative learning. I've watched children play repetitiously day after day in a prestructured domestic play area. When we introduced large blocks instead of the usual sink, cupboard, and stove, the children made their own innovative equipment as needed. Their play then evolved; it became more imaginative and complex; it required more information. The children asked more questions and were eager to find answers, which led to group discussion, books, trips, and child-devised experiments, not only with blocks but also in drawing, in painting, and at the water table. The children's involvement drew playmates into the large block area like magic until one day Judy complained to me:

"Even Eric wants in. There's just not room."

"Maybe he could stop by as a salesman?"

"We don't need a thing."

"A distant cousin? . . . " At this Judy left me, with a glint in her eye.

"OK, Eric," she said. "You *can* play with us. You'll be Cousin Edward. You just died of cancer, and we'll have a *lovely* funeral. Molly, you paint some flowers; Josh, you dig the grave; and that will take care of that."

Eric, far from being deceased, asked, "Wha'd'ya know about fun'rals?"

"Don't even think about it. You're dead."

"Well, I'm having a 'pensive casket."

* * *

Rules for play with large blocks

1. Take out blocks only as needed.

2. Build with care. No crashing, throwing, or dropping blocks.

3. Don't use equipment to threaten or hit someone.

4. Don't use another child's blocks without her or his permission.

5. Stack away all equipment at cleanup time.

6. Stick to the rules, or don't use the blocks. (This is the only punishment needed. It works because the dangers are easy to see, peer pressure is palpable, and the children so love block activity.)

Large-block dramatic play differs from play with unit blocks

These two forms of block play differ, just as the child's life-size world differs from the world of small toys. Child-life-size dramatic play often is close, personal, and subjectively compelling, and it involves the whole child. In contrast, the microworld of unit blocks allows the child to manipulate a number of small toys at a distance. Involvement is less personal, and the child often sees a total situation with actual, physical perspective. Unit blocks and toys also become concrete *symbols* for real life. As such, they provide the child with practice for the more abstract, written-word symbols that come later in reading. On the other hand, large-block dramatic play, in which the child herself is a participant, gives that immediate, holistic experience that conveys its own effective insight.

While at Harvard I did a study of children's ways of coping near the end of a 10-hour child care program. By late afternoon, 4- and 5-year-olds, who had been in the program since 7 A.M., usually were tired, intractable, and tearful. We tried everything from longer rest periods to art, table games, unit blocks, large blocks, cooking, snacks, reading aloud, and storytelling. What worked? Large blocks. The children often built houses, tunnels, or dens into which they could retire quietly alone—or with a buddy—away from many children, away from adults.

All in all, creative learning with large blocks lights a child's lively curiosity, that marvelous innate drive toward knowing. Involvement is contagious. The children build together with shared purpose, with shared pain and laughter, with hard work and deep satisfaction.

Learning with Large Blocks: Values and Goals

In today's environment of disenchantment with much in education, we teachers need to clarify our values and goals for children. We need to articulate how each aspect of our classroom—in this instance, use of large blocks—promotes optimum individual development within a democratic society. Through their inventive building and dramatic play with large blocks, young children begin to realize these goals in their classroom—in their own child community. Means and ends become one.

These VALUES underlie goals for children in large-block experiences:

- to trust, respect, and support each individual as a unique and inestimable human being whose innate capacities to learn through self-initiative are the very essence of good education in school, as in life;
- to help children realize their full creative potential, not only for individual development but for group learning;
- to support deep, often unconscious feelings of self-esteem, not only directly but particularly through child-group appreciation of individual contribution in all its diversity, a support better felt than formalized;
- to foster both self-reliance and self-propelled cooperation, with joy in the synergy of group endeavor;
- to foster peaceful solutions through planning and working together with sensitive help to others rather than through competition;
- to foster acquisition of both rational and intuitive knowledge of one's self and one's world with imagination, integrity, tolerance (humility and forgiveness), generosity, compassion, joy, and humor;
- to foster knowledge, caring, joy, and wonder in nature with its interdependence and unity of which we are part; and
- to value process more than product, to realize the harmony between means and ends, and to know the similarity—regardless of aims—between method and result.

These large-block GOALS are reached at each child's singular pace:

Physical
- good health, with awareness of and joy in it and increasing knowledge of its maintenance;
- development and coordination of small and, especially, large muscles;
- achievement of an instant, dimensional sense of oneself in space;
- a deft, intuitional awareness of object-space relationships; and
- a feeling of joy and competence in motor control, rhythm, and balance.

Social
- joy and skill in cooperative play and work in both leading and following roles;
- ability and informed loyalty in following group rules;

- acceptance and respect of diversity among children and adults;
- achievement of satisfying friendships with compassion;
- a sense of responsibility for the group and the self-esteem so gained;
- joy in group (community) accomplishment;
- a deeply felt awareness that authority and group structure should promote individual fulfillment;
- building intuitive relationships with confidence; and
- pleasure and competence in effective communication—talking, listening, and reflecting the value of others' thinking.

Cognitive

- development of relationship thinking—cause-and-effect and the relatedness of objects, ideas, feelings, and activities;
- concrete use of counting and one-to-one correspondence, awareness and use of simple shapes and of single-attribute classification, functional awareness of simple fractions and multiples of the large blocks in daily use, and use of balance, bridging, and cantilever in building;
- affection and respect for books as a source of expanding one's information, pleasure, and vision in large-block play;
- knowledge and use of other creative activities (such as drawing, painting, clay, music, dance, and drama) in relation to large-block experience, with child purpose and satisfaction;
- increased joy and skill in discovery, in *active* learning, in striving to find information needed for one's own purpose in large-block experience—a purpose that is often realized as a contribution to the group;
- a growing perception of large-block play as symbolic of the child's real world—a cognitive perspective of its value not only for confronting life but also for reading readiness, which requires increasing intellectual grasp and use of symbols; and
- the ability to recognize and value one's own and others' intuitive knowledge—an important quality in today's computer-information age, when linear thinking too readily overrules intuition and holistic sensitivity.

Emotional

- development toward personality integration;
- strong, positive feelings about self in many roles and skills;
- the ability to meet new situations with resourcefulness;
- the ability to sustain interest and overcome frustration;
- openness and sensitivity to an array of feelings in oneself and in others, such as humor, sadness, joy, tension, anger, excitement, peace, compassion, etc., and appropriate, conscious self-awareness and control; and
- joy and vitality toward an intuitive/rational and loving view of one's social and physical worlds.

Appendix 1

Stages of Block Building

Whether children are introduced to blocks at the age of 2 or at the age of 6, they seem to pass through all the stages (except Stage 1) described by Harriet Johnson. The only difference is that older children go through the early stages much more quickly and arrive at a stage more appropriate for their age.

* * *

The material in this appendix is based on Harriet Johnson's *The Art of Block Building* (chapter 2) and was condensed by Maja Apelman.

STAGE 1. Blocks are carried around, not used for construction. This stage applies to the very young child.

STAGE 2. Building begins. Children make mostly rows, either horizontal (on the floor) or vertical (stacked). There is much repetition in this early building pattern.

143

STAGE **3**. Bridging—two blocks with
a space between them, connected
by a third block—is used.

STAGE 4. Enclosures—blocks placed in such a way that they enclose a space—are made. Bridging and enclosures are among the earliest technical building problems that children have to solve. They occur soon after a child begins to use blocks regularly.

145

STAGE 5. With age, children become steadily more facile and imaginative in their block building. They use more blocks and create more elaborate designs, using pattern and balance.

Stage 6. *Naming of structures for dramatic play begins. Before this stage, children also may have named their structures, but the names were not necessarily related to the function of the building.*

147

Stage 7. Block buildings often reproduce or symbolize actual structures the children know, and there is a strong impulse toward dramatic play around the block structures.

Appendix 2

Suggested Equipment for Block Building

Set of blocks for a group of 15 to 20 children (numbers in parentheses refer to drawing at right)

Number of blocks recommended for this age group			
	3 years	**4 years**	**5 years**
half units (1)	72	82	96
units (2)	180	192	250
double units (3)	140	152	200
quadruple units (4)	48	48	64
pillars (5)	32	64	80
small cylinders (6)	20	32	40
large cylinders (7)	20	24	32
circular curves (8)	12	16	16
elliptical curves (9)	8	16	16
pairs of small triangles (10)	16	22	36
pairs of large triangles (11)	16	32	36
floor boards—11" (12)	12	26	50
roof boards—22" (not illustrated)	0	12	20
ramps (13)	8	12	16
right-angle switches (14) and/or X switches (not illustrated)	0	4	8
half pillars (not illustrated)	0	12	16
Y switches (15)	2	2	4

From *Play Equipment for the Nursery School* by Jessie Stanton, Alma Weisberg, and the faculty of the Bank Street School for Children, 1962, rev. ed. New York: Bank Street College of Education.

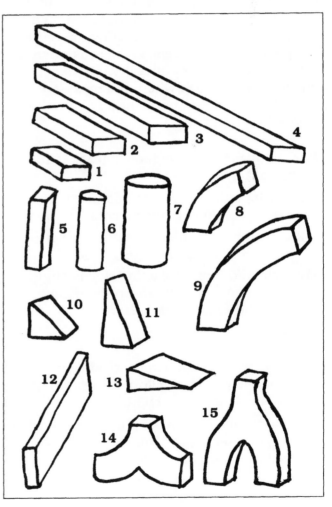

As children have more experience with blocks, greater varieties and quantities may be needed. Four-year-olds who have used blocks actively for a year or two, for example, will often use even more blocks than are suggested for 5-year-olds.

Block accessories

(From Stanton et al. 1962)

The materials suggested below demonstrate the range of materials children use to augment not only the block buildings but also their play with the structures. While the figures, animals, and vehicles are sufficiently varied to fulfill children's more recurrent themes, often a child's keen observation and commitment to realistic detail require other supplementary materials. There is often a deeper satisfaction and a greater variety of imaginative themes when materials are suggestive of many uses rather than of a single function.

Rubber, plastic, or wooden figures (adults about 5" high)

2 varying ethnic families: mother, father, boy, girl, baby, grandparents

12 community figures: farmers, workers, doctors, firefighters, etc.

16 farm and domestic animals: cow, bull, calf, 2 horses, colt, sheep, ram, lamb, 2 pigs, piglets, cat, dog, etc.

1 set zoo animals

Vehicles (plastic, rubber, or wood is recommended for younger children; round-edged metal is safe for older children)

2 sets trains and tracks (for older children), 2 sets interlocking trains or sandtrains (for younger children)

24 small cars, airplanes, buses, assorted trucks, and tractor (according to environment). Axles should be enclosed to prevent loss of wheels.

4 jumbo trucks (if floor space permits)

6 small and large boats (tugboats, barges, liners, ferries, etc., according to environment)

Additional accessories

Adapted from *Blockbuilding: Some Practical Suggestions for Teachers* by Maja Apelman, n.d. New York University, Project Head Start In-Service Training Program. Mimeographed. Used by permission.

Colored cubes are often considered part of the basic block accessories. Children love to decorate buildings with them. Any incomplete set of small blocks such as paquetry blocks or large dominoes should be saved for the block corner. Also, any other assortment of odd small blocks or spools may be put into boxes for decorative use with buildings.

For 5-year-olds and older:

Samples of tiles, linoleum squares, rugs. Children like to cover floor areas and walls of buildings and make decorative patterns with these.

Shells, such as scallop or clam shells. They can be used for plates when a child builds a restaurant (with food made of plasticine) or for decorative purposes.

Pebbles, small stones, little sticks for cargo on trains, boats, and trucks. Children can collect these on walks to a nearby park.

A variety of small containers. These are useful for all sorts of things, such as keeping money in a store or providing water for animals in a farm or zoo.

A variety of lumber scraps, especially flat pieces. They are used for roofs, wide bridges, etc.

Furniture. Keep items very simple. They can be made at the woodworking bench. (Commercially bought furniture is either very expensive or very flimsy!) Children, however, also should be shown how to improvise furniture from the blocks themselves.

Familiar signs, such as "One Way," "School Crossing," "Bus Stop," etc.

Tongue depressors for attaching signs or making fences. They will stand up if stuck into a small piece of plasticine.

Thin pieces of rubber tubing. Tacked to a cylinder block, they can make a simple gas pump. Children will think of other uses.

Excelsior. It makes good hay for farm animals.

Trees. Construction is simple: Let the child draw a tree, cut it out, then staple it to a tongue depressor and stick it into a piece of plasticine so it will stand up.

Dry-cell batteries with lights.

Any old piece of machinery, especially if it has switches or knobs that turn. An old TV antenna, a broken clock, earphones, or a radio will be used by the children in countless ways. Be sure to remove hazardous parts.

Magazine pictures of bridges, roads, constructions, or city scenes. Mount them on cardboard and have them available for individual children who may need clarification when reconstructing something they have seen. Display the pictures on walls in your block area if your room layout permits this.

Signs. Children love to have signs written for their buildings. If saved and stored in a simple manner, they can be used again, and children may begin to recognize some of them. This is an excellent early reading activity.

Five-year-olds are very capable and independent. If manila and colored construction paper, a few crayons, scissors, masking tape, and string are always available in or near the block corner, the children will begin to make their own signs and draw trees, people, and other things they need, thereby using their imagination in a constructive, purposeful way.

Note: The above lists are simply suggestions. Obviously, no teacher will ever put out all these accessories at once. However, the larger your supply of odds and ends, the better you will be able to help the children in the block corner when they begin to need accessories for specific purposes.

Block storage

(From Stanton et al. 1962)

Block cabinets should be sturdy, on a 3" baseboard, made of ¾" x 12" lumber, with a solid back, and divided into cubicles for orderly storage. The overall dimensions for a block cabinet for fifteen 3-year-olds might be 4'6" wide x 3' high.

Cubicles should be 11¾" high, with small cubicles (13" wide) for half units, cylinders, ramps, floor boards, and pillars; medium cubicles (18" wide) for trains, cube boxes, triangles, switches, curves, arches, small cars, and boats; large cubicles (24"–37" wide) for units, double units, quadruple units, roof boards, animals, people, and other accessories.

Blocks should be presented on shelves in such a way that their mathematical relationships can be perceived in terms of sizes and categories of shapes. They should be arranged with the following considerations:

• Large blocks and large vehicles should be near the bottom for safety in removal and for proper weighting of the cabinet.

• Each shape and type of accessory should have its own space for easier location and orderly pickup.

• Where quantity is sufficient, the most popular shapes (units, double units, quadruple units) should be divided to encourage building in front of different parts of the shelving. Younger children and novices tend to build immediately in front of the shelves.

• Longer and lower cabinets (or two smaller cabinets) help to disperse the areas in which children build.

Bibliography

Antin, C. 1952. *Blocks in the curriculum.* New York: Early Childhood Education Council of New York City.

Apelman, M. n.d. *Block building: Some practical suggestions for teachers.* New York University, Project Head Start In-Service Training Program. Mimeographed.

Baroody, A.J. 1987. *Children's mathematical thinking: A developmental framework for preschool, primary, and special education teachers.* New York: Teachers College Press.

Bearison, D. 1982. New directions in studies of social interaction and cognitive growth. In *Social cognitive development in context,* ed. F. Serafica. New York: Guilford.

Beeson, B., & A. Williams. 1979. *A study of sex stereotyping in child-selected play activities of preschool children.* ERIC, ED 186102.

Beeson, B., & A. Williams. 1980. *A study of sex stereotyping in child-selected play activities of preschool children.* ERIC, ED 201390.

Bender, J. 1978. Large hollow blocks: Relationship of quantity to block building behaviors. *Young Children* 33 (6): 17–23. Also in *Ideas that work with children,* Vol. 2, 1979, eds. L. Adams & B. Garlick, 140–46. Washington, DC: NAEYC.

Biber, B. 1951. Play as a growth process. *Vassar Alumnae Magazine* 37 (2).

Biber, B. 1959. Premature structuring as a deterrent to creativity. *American Journal of Orthopsychiatry* 29 (2).

Biber, B. 1967. A learning-teaching paradigm integrating intellectual and affective processes. In *Behavioral Science Frontiers in Education,* eds. E.M. Bower & W.G. Hollister. New York: Wiley.

Biber, B., & M.B. Franklin. 1967. Relevance of developmental and psychodynamic concepts to the education of the preschool child. *Journal of the American Academy of Child Psychiatry* 6 (1): 5–24.

Bobrow, D.G., & A.M. Collins, eds. 1975. *Representation and understanding: Studies in cognitive science.* New York: Academic Press.

Bransford, J.D., J. Barclay, & J. Frank. 1972. Sentence memory: A constructive versus an interpretive approach. *Cognitive Psychology* 3: 193–210.

Bransford, J.D., & N.S. McCarrell. 1974. A sketch of a cognitive approach to comprehension: Some thoughts about understanding what it means to comprehend. In *Cognition and the symbolic processes,* eds. W.B. Weimer & D.S. Palermo. Hillsdale, NJ: Lawrence Erlbaum.

Bredekamp, S., ed. 1987. *Developmentally appropriate practice in early childhood programs serving children from birth through age 8.* Exp. ed. Washington, DC: NAEYC.

Burkhart, D.H. 1993. Building blocks, building skills. *Pre-K Today* 7 (7).

Burton, G.M. 1985. *Towards a good beginning: Teaching early childhood mathematics.* Menlo Park, CA: Addison-Wesley.

Cartwright, S. 1988. Play can be the building blocks of learning. *Young Children* 43 (5): 44–47.

Cartwright, S. 1990. Learning with large blocks. *Young Children* 45 (3): 38–41.

Cartwright, S. 1995. Block play: Experiences in cooperative learning and living. *Child Care Information Exchange* (May): 39–41.

Charney, R., M.K. Clayton, & C. Wood. 1990. *Bringing blocks back to the classroom.* Greenfield, MA: Northeast Foundation for Children.

Church, E.B., & K. Miller. 1990. *Learning through play: Blocks: A practical guide for teaching young children.* New York: Scholastic.

Churchill, E.M. 1961. *Counting and measuring: An approach to number education in the infant school.* Toronto: University of Toronto Press.

Clayton, M.K. 1989. *Places to start: Implementing the developmental classroom.* Greenfield, MA: Northeast Foundation for Children.

Copeland, R.W. 1984. *How children learn mathematics: Teaching implications of Piaget's research.* New York: Macmillan.

Craycroft, R. 1986. Construction toys and architectural values. In *Building block art*, ed. P.H. Sperr. Philadelphia: Please Touch Museum.

Creative Associates. 1979. Blocks: A creative curriculum for early childhood. Author.

Cruikshank, D.E., D.L. Fitzgerald, & L.R. Jensen. 1980. *Young children learn mathematics*. Boston: Allyn & Bacon.

Cuffaro, H.K. 1986. The development of block building. In *Building block art*, ed. P.H. Sperr. Philadelphia: Please Touch Museum.

Cuffaro, H.K. 1991. A view of materials as texts of the early childhood curriculum. In *Issues in early childhood curriculum: Yearbook in early childhood education*. Vol. 2, eds. B. Spodek & O.N. Saracho. New York: Teachers College Press.

Cuffaro, H.K. 1995. Block building: Opportunities for learning. *Child Care Information Exchange* (May): 36–38.

Dewey, J. 1963. *Experience and education*. London: Collier Macmillan.

Dienes, Z.P., & E.W. Golding. 1966. *Exploration of space and practical measurements*. New York: Herder & Herder.

Dodge, D.T., & L.J. Colker. 1992. Why blocks are important. In *The creative curriculum for early childhood*. 3d ed. Washington, DC: Teaching Strategies.

Dodge, D.T., & J. Phinney. 1990. *The creative curriculum*. Washington, DC: Teaching Strategies. Videocassette.

Dodge, D.T., & J. Phinney. 1990. *The creative curriculum for early childhood*. 3d ed. Washington, DC: Teaching Strategies.

Erikson, E.H. 1950. *Childhood and society*. New York: Norton.

Erikson, E.H. 1959. Identity and the life cycle. *Psychological issues* 1 (1).

Erikson, E. 1977. *Toys and reasons: Stages in the ritualization of experience*. New York: Norton.

Farrell. M. 1957. Sex differences in block play in the early childhood. *Journal of Educational Research* 51: 281–84.

Feeney, L. 1993. Building blocks, skills, and togetherness. *Pre-K Today* 7 (7).

Forman, G.E. 1982. A search for the origins of equivalence concepts through microanalysis of block-play. In *Action and thought: From sensorimotor schemes to symbolic operations*, ed. G.E. Forman. New York: Academic Press.

Frank, L.K. 1955. Play in personality development. *American Journal of Orthopsychiatry* 23 (3): 576–90.

Garvey, C. 1990. *Play*. Enlarged ed. Cambridge, MA: Harvard University Press.

Gehlbach, R.D. 1991. Play, Piaget, and creativity: The promise of design. *Journal of Creative Behavior* 25 (2): 137–44.

Gelfer, J.I., & P.G. Perkins. 1988. Using blocks to build art concepts: A new look at an old friend. *Early Child Development and Care* 30: 59–69.

Goodson, B.D. 1982. The development of hierarchic organization: The reproduction, planning, and perception of multiarch block structures. In *Action and thought: From sensorimotor schemes to symbolic operations*, ed. G.E. Forman. New York: Academic Press.

Green, V.P., & L. Schaefer. 1984. Preschool teachers play materials preference. *Early Child Development and Care* 14 (1–2): 85–92.

Griffiths, R. 1935. *Imagination in early childhood*. London: Routledge & Kegan Paul.

Guanella, F. 1934. Blockbuilding activities of young children. *Archives of Psychology* 174: 1–92.

Hartley, R., L. Frank, & R. Goldenson. 1952. *Understanding children's play*. New York: Columbia University Press.

Herman, J. 1986. Building block art: A guide for parents and teachers. In *Building block art*, ed. P.H. Sperr. Philadelphia: Please Touch Museum.

Herron, R.E., & B. Sutton-Smith. 1971. *Child's play*. New York: Wiley.

Hirsch, E.S. n.d. *Transition periods: Stumbling blocks of education*. New York: Early Childhood Education Council of New York City.

Holloway, G.E.T. 1967. *An introduction to the child's conception of space*. New York: Humanities Press.

Hulson & Reich. 1931. Blocks and the four-year-old. *Childhood Education* 8: 66–68.

Isaacs, S. 1948. The nature and function of phantasy. *International Journal of Psychoanalysis* 29 (part 2): 73–96.

Isaacs, S. 1966. *Intellectual growth in young children*. New York: Schocken.

Isaacs, S. 1972. *Social development on young children*. New York: Schocken.

Isbell, R.T., & S.C. Raines. 1991. Young children's oral language production in three types of play centers. *Journal of Research in Childhood Education* 5 (2): 140–46.

Johnson, H. [1928] 1972. *Children in the nursery school*. New York: Agathon.

Karges-Bone, L. 1991. Blocks are not (circle all): Messy, expensive, difficult. *Dimensions* 20 (1): 5–8.

Kinsmans, C.A., & L.E. Berk. 1979. Joining the block and housekeeping areas: Changes in play and social behavior. *Young Children* 35 (1): 66–75.

Kintsch, W., & T.A. Van Dijk. 1978. Toward a model of text comprehension and production. *Psychological Review* 84 (5): 363–94.

Koepke, M. 1989. Learning by the block. *Teacher Magazine* (December).

Leeb-Lundberg, K. 1970. Kindergarten mathematics laboratory. *The Arithmetic Teacher* 17 (5): 372–86.

Leeb-Lundberg, K. 1972. Friedrich Froebel's mathematics for the kindergarten: Philosophy, program, and implementation in the United States. Ph.D. diss., New York University.

Leeb-Lundberg, K. 1985. *Mathematics is more than counting*. Washington, DC: Association for Childhood Education International.

Lovell, K. 1964. *The growth of basic mathematical and scientific concepts in children*. London: University of London Press.

Lovell, K. 1971. *The growth of understanding in mathematics: Kindergarten through grade three*. New York: Holt, Rinehart, & Winston.

Lowenfeld, M. 1967. *Play in childhood*. New York: Wiley, Science Editions.

Massey, M. 1969. Kindergarten children's behavior in block building situation. Ph.D. diss., Florida State University.

McCracken, J.B. 1987. *More than 1, 2, 3: The real basics of mathematics*. Washington, DC: NAEYC.

Millar, S. 1969. *The psychology of play*. London: Pelican.

Mitchell, L.S. 1951. *Our children and our schools*. New York: Simon & Schuster.

Mitchell, L.S. 1971. *Young geographers*. New York: Agathon.

Moffitt, M.M. 1970. *Blocks: A medium for perceptual learning*. New York: Campus Films. Videocassette.

Moffitt, M.M. 1971. *Block building*. Washington, DC: Childhood Resources.

Moyer, K., & B. Gilner. 1981. *The development of symbolic representation: The case of building blocks*. ERIC, ED 200333.

Murray, J.W. 1978. The children build a city. In *The City and Country School: Selected talks and articles*, ed. M. Speer, 37–43. New York: City and Country School.

Nourot, P.M., & J.L. Van Hoorn. 1991. Symbolic play in preschool and primary settings. *Young Children* 46 (6): 40–48.

Piaget, J. 1955. *The child's construction of reality*. London: Routledge & Kegan Paul.

Piaget, J. 1962. *Play, dreams, and imitation in childhood*. New York: W.W. Norton.

Piaget, J. 1962. *Science of education and the psychology of the child*. New York: Viking.

Piaget, J. 1967. *The child's conception of numbers*. New York: W.W. Norton.

Piaget, J., & B. Inhelder. 1967. *The child's conception of space*. London: Routledge & Kegan Paul.

Piaget, J., & B. Inhelder. 1969. *The psychology of the child*. London: Routledge & Kegan Paul.

Piaget, J., B. Inhelder, & A. Szeminska. 1964. *The child's conception of geometry*. New York: Harper & Row.

Pratt, C., ed. 1924. *Experimental practice in the City and Country School*. New York: E.P. Dutton.

Pratt, C. [1948] 1970. *I learn from children*. New York: Cornerstone Library. New edition, 1990. New York: Harper & Row, Perennial Library.

Pratt, C. 1973. The play school. In *Experimental schools revisited*, ed. C. Winsor. New York: Agathon.

Pratt, C., & J. Stanton. 1926. *Before books*. New York: Adelphi.

Provenzo, E.F., Jr., & A. Brett. 1983. *The complete block book*. Syracuse, NY: Syracuse University Press.

Reifel, S. 1982. The structure and content of early representational play: The case of building blocks. In *Young children and their families: Needs of the nineties*, eds. S. Hill & B.J. Barnes. Lexington, MA: DC Heath.

Reifel, S. 1983. Take a closer look at block play. *Texas Child Care Quarterly* 7 (1).

Reifel, S. 1984. Block construction: Children's developmental landmarks in representation of space. *Young Children* 40 (1): 61–67.

Reifel, S. 1984. Symbolic representation at two ages: Block building of a story. *Discourse Processes* 7: 11–20.

Reifel, S. 1995. Enriching the possibilities of block play. *Child Care Information Exchange* (May): 48–50.

Reifel, S. In press. Play: Bases for literacy. In *Achieving school readiness: Public libraries and the first of the National Education Goals*, eds. B.F. Immroth & V. Ash-Geisler. Chicago: American Library Association.

Reifel, S., & P.M. Greenfield. 1982. Structural development in symbolic medium: The representational use of block construction. In *Action and thought: From sensorimotor schemes to symbolic operations*, ed. G.E. Forman. New York: Academic Press.

Reifel, S., & P.M. Greenfield. 1983. Part-whole relations: Some structural features of children's representational block play. *Child Care Quarterly* 12 (1).

Reifel, S., & J. Yeatman. 1991. Action, talk and thought in the block corner: Developmental trends. In *Play and the social context of development in early care and education*, eds. B. Scales, M. Almy, A. Nicolopoulou, & S. Ervin-Tripp. New York: Teachers College Press.

Ripple, R.E., & V.N. Rockcastle, eds. 1964. *Piaget rediscovered*. Ithaca, NY: Conference on Cognitive Studies and Curriculum Development, Cornell University and University of California.

Robinson, E.L. 1958. The form and imaginative content of children's block building. Ph.D. diss., University of Minnesota.

Rogers, D.L. 1987. Fostering social development through block play. *Day Care and Early Education* (Spring).

Rubin, K. 1977. The social and cognitive value of preschool toys and activities. *Canadian Journal of Behavioral Science* 9: 382–85.

Rumelhart, D., & A. Ortory. 1977. The representation of knowledge in memory. In *Schooling and the acquisition of knowledge*, eds. R. Anderson, R. Spiro, & W. Montagne. Hillsdale, NJ: Lawrence Erlbaum.

Saunders, R., & A.M. Bingham-Newman. 1984. *Piagetian perspective for preschools: A thinking book for teachers*. Englewood Cliffs, NJ: Prentice-Hall.

Sawyers, J.K. 1989. Constructive play: Ideas in the works. *Pre-K Today* 3 (2).

Schirrmacher, R. 1975. Effects of adult modeling on the developmental level of children's block construction measured on an ordinal scale. Ph.D. diss., University of Illinois.

Shapiro, E., & B. Biber. 1972. The education of young children: A developmental-interaction approach. *The Teachers College Record* 74 (1).

Singer, R. 1988. Estimation and counting in the block corner. *Arithmetic Teacher* 35 (5): 10–14.

Sperr, P.H., ed. 1986. *Building block art*. Philadelphia: Please Touch Museum.

Stanton, J., A. Weisberg, and the faculty of Bank Street School for Children. 1962. *Play equipment for the nursery school*. New York: Bank Street College of Education.

Starks, E.B. 1970. *Blockbuilding*. Washington, DC: American Association of Elementary and Kindergarten-Nursery Education.

Stea, D., & J.M. Blant. 1973. Notes toward a development theory of spatial learning. In *Image and Environment: Cognitive mapping and spatial behavior*, eds. R.M. Downs & D. Dtea. Chicago: Aldine.

Stephens, K. 1991. *Block adventures, building creativity and concepts through block play*. Weston, MA: First Teacher Press.

Stephens, K. 1995. On the floor with kids: Teachers as block play partners. *Child Care Information Exchange* (May): 51–53.

Stritzel, K. 1995. Block play is for ALL children. *Child Care Information Exchange* (May) 42–47.

Sutton-Smith, B. 1971. The playful modes of knowing. In *Play: The child strives toward self realization*, ed. G. Engstrom. Washington, DC: NAEYC.

Tegano, D.W., J.D. Moran, & J.K. Sawyers. 1991. *Creativity in early childhood classrooms*. Washington, DC: National Education Association.

Ushiyama, T., T. Shimian, & M. Takahashi. 1974. Interaction process of two children. *The Japanese Journal of Educational Psychology* 22: 176–80.

Varma, M. 1980. Sex stereotyping and block play of preschool children. *Indian Educational Review* (July): 32–37.

Vezeeken, P. 1961. *Spatial development: Constructive praxia from birth to age of seven*. Croningen, The Netherlands: Walters.

Wadsworth, B.J. 1989. *Piaget's theory of cognitive and affective development*. 4th ed. New York: Longman.

Wassermann, S. 1992. Serious play in the classroom. *Childhood Education* 68 (3): 133–38.

Winsor, C., ed. 1973. *Experimental schools revisited*. New York: Agathon.

Wright, F.L. 1932. *An autobiography*. New York: Longman Green.

Subject Index

Author Index